A Criminal Waste of Time

A Criminal Waste of Time

William W. Bedsworth

Recorder Books/American Lawyer Media

SAN FRANCISCO, CALIFORNIA

Illustrations by Mark Ziemann

Edited by: Scott Graham and Greg Mitchell

Book production designers: David Chin, Tess Herrmann, Tim Williams

Proofed by: Candice McFarland and Kathleen McBride

Printed in the United States of America

ISBN 1-58852-122-2

For Kelly

who somehow understands

contents

contents

It was a bench trial in a government contract case involving some newfangled conveyor-driven equipment for sorting mail in a cavernous facility of the United States Postal Service. The witness was droning on about how the equipment would fail on a regular basis, apparently because too much hydraulic pressure caused pipes to burst, resulting in leaks.

Suddenly the lawyer at the opposing counsel's table sprang to his feet. "Oh darn," I thought to myself. "He's going to make an objection. Now I'll have to figure out what the witness was actually trying to tell me so I don't look like an idiot."

"Your honor," the lawyer said, clearing his throat, "talking about too much hydraulic pressure and the risk of leaks, could we have a short recess?"

I had heard such requests dozens of times, but never in such picturesque form. I granted the recess and eventually went on with the trial, still shaking my head. It was only years later, when I tried to tell the story to a friend, that it dawned on me I should have gotten a transcript; it's the kind of story that is much better told if you can quote the actual words — and provide a transcript as proof that it really happened just as you described it. But by then I had moved to another court and it was much too late.

Quaint incidents like this happen in the law — and in life — all the time. But most of us, judges especially, are dolts when it comes to noticing such gems and preserving them for posterity. It takes a keen eye, and a sharp wit, to identify those little absurdities that crop up in all human endeavors. And it takes real talent and skill — and an affinity for the preposterous — to present the incident in just the right light so the reader or listener will immediately see the silliness of it and surrender a laugh.

Making people laugh is hard, and getting much harder in a world where every new joke — are there really any new jokes left? — circumnavigates the globe seven times before those of us in the Pacific time zone have read our morning e-mail.

What people actually do in their daily lives turns out to be the last reliable supply of mirth left to us. Stories that would get only a nervous titter if invented, become knee-slappers if you are convinced that they really happened; verisimilitude exponentially increases to the humor value of any anecdote.

No one I know is better than William Bedsworth — Beds, as everyone calls him — at finding the humorous, the absurd, the odd, the bizarre or the just plain screwy among the incidents of daily life. And no one quite has his knack for stripping them of all pretense and exposing their essential funniness. He's been doing just that for the past two decades and now some of his best columns have been collected in this book. If you are holding it in your hand — as you no doubt must be — just start turning pages and get ready for a treat.

Oh, and don't forget the footnotes; they're often the best part.

— *Alex Kozinski*

introduction

I've been practicing law for 33 years. And for 22 of those years, I've been venting random thoughts out of the boiler of my brain through the safety valve of my monthly humor column. Both numbers flat-out flabbergast me.

Like most baby boomers, my sense of time has been badly distorted. Television, radio, jet planes, warp speed communication, instant replay, DVDs, and now the Internet have turned time into something so malleable that it has largely lost its meaning.

In the course of five minutes, I can turn on the History Channel and relive the Kennedy assassination from 40 years ago; turn to ESPN to see Todd Walker's home run from 40 seconds ago hit the foul pole six different times from three different angles; and talk to my son in Japan, where it's already late Monday afternoon as I sit down to watch "60 Minutes." Tomorrow I will fly to Hawaii, landing at almost the same time I took off, even though I've traveled 2,600 miles; on the way to the airport, I will listen to "Hotel California" — 40 minutes spent deep in the '80s.

The upshot of all this temporal dysphasia is not just that I can't figure out where the time went. Heck, that's nothing new: Job took time to complain, "My days are swifter than a weaver's shuttle," and Job had a lot to complain about.[1] So this, "Where'd all the time go?" jeremiad may be older than Jeremiah.

But what bugs me isn't that I'm standing out here in the River of Time with entirely too much of it downstream from me. That I could deal with — at least as well as I deal with anything.

No, what bugs me is that I seem to be stuck in some bizarre little eddy where weird stuff circles around me like leaves unable to get back into the current. Every day lawyers float past me with newspapers open to stories about presidential debates and stock quotes and new legislation. And every day I read the same newspapers and find stories about the Lord High Chancellor's wallpaper allowance (page 133) and men who smuggle monkeys in their pants (page 143) and sell seal penises (page 69).[2]

Lawyers come into my court with cases about wrongful termination

---

1 - He also appears to have had access to a weaver's shuttle, whatever that is.

2 - These are different men; I think I'd feel better if just one maniac was doing both these things, but such is not the way of our world.

and breach of the covenant of good faith. I listen attentively. But other judges are dealing with patents on peanut butter and jelly sandwiches (page 159) and sex on the sixth green (page 7) and whether aliens from outer space should be granted copyrights (page 97).

And the really disturbing thing is that the mainstream floaters don't seem to know this stuff is going on. I write from my little whirlpool about flying pigs (page 123) and silent music (page 92)[3] and the lawyers out in the channel ask me where I get this stuff. They float by in their Lexi and BMWs[4], apparently oblivious to the fact I'm taking on all the nuttiness in the judicial cosmos in my own personal Charybdis of lucidity. It hardly seems fair.

Yet once a month, as a public service, I post my little dispatches in legal newspapers all over the country, warning les habitants du droit of the surely impending apocalypse. I'm the legal equivalent of the guy who walks around with the sandwich board that says, "Repent; the end is nigh."

Nobody repents. I get pretty much the same response as the sandwich board guy: a couple of smiles, a rueful chuckle or two and a lot of head-shaking. I might as well be talking to Pacific pocket mice (page 112).[5]

It's discouraging. I feel like Upton Sinclair, who, lamenting the success of his classic novel, "The Jungle," said, "I aimed at the heart of America and hit its stomach." I seem to have aimed at Upton Sinclair and hit Bobcat Goldthwaite.

But I will not be deterred. I will trudge on. It's a mission for me. I've taken an oath as a justice of the Court of Appeal.[6] And I'm not about to give up.

Not as long as there are giant, man-eating wombats from the planet Zangor living in Justice Rehnquist's rec room.

---

3 - Good luck getting your head around that one.

4 - OK, the metaphor's starting to break down now, but you get my drift.

5 - Who, as it turns out, are a lot better off financially than most of the lawyers — and all of the judges — I know.

6 - Actually, I have no idea what this has to do with anything, but it kinda has a ring to it, don't you think?

Getting a Leg Up on Science

Compute the damages in this case and earn MCLE credits for headache endurance.

I am the guy Arthur C. Clarke had in mind when he said, "We have reached the point in man's development where any reasonably advanced technology is indistinguishable from magic." I am no more capable of coping with the 21st century than George III would have been. And every day, the newspapers insist on reminding me of this.

I am a technopeasant. The Lord of the Manor may understand PET scans and DNA and the Internet, but to me and my fellow serfs, it's all magic. So help me, if somebody showed up at my door tomorrow with a tank truck and said he was there to refill the electricity reservoir, I'd let him into the basement and get out my checkbook.

That's how I became a lawyer. I know it's different now, but in the mid-'60s, when I was planning my life, it was pretty simple. If you were a smart kid who wasn't good at math or science, they stamped pre-law on your college application and moved on to the next kid. If I'd had a decent high school guidance counselor, I'd be doing play-by-play for the Visalia Oaks today.

Unbeknownst to me, I wasn't so much failing to understand Algebra II as I was getting a leg up on Remedies. You can draw a straight line from the B-minus I got in chemistry (a catastrophe of tsunamic proportion at the time) to my present position, where my inability to distinguish exothermic from endothermic reactions is almost never noticed.[1]

But every so often, I'm required to deal with the world in which I live. Every now and again, the third millennium rears its ugly head and I have to deal with cases that involve technology more challenging than doorknobs and dumbwaiters. Always with untoward results.

I mention this now because my newspaper today is just chockfull of frightening scientific news from other parts of the country, and I'm scared to death it's going to spread to California and end up on my docket.[2] According to the Reuters news service, "An Alaska woman, shocked to receive part of her dead father's leg in the mail instead of the gourmet LobsterGram she was expecting, has filed suit against the Houston, Texas, firm that sent it, alleging mental anguish."

And well she might. Certainly that sounds like something that might induce mental anguish.

Seems LaMara Lane opened what she thought was a food gift sent to her North Pole, Alaska[3], home and found instead ... well, to use the scientific term[4], the fibula paterfamilias.

"How," you're probably asking yourself, "could something like

---

[1] At least not to my face.

[2] Although I will forward all the scientific folderol to our newest justice, Ray Ikola, who has both bachelor's and master's degrees in mechanical engineering and a Ph.D. in electrophysics. He was a little nonplussed the other day when I asked if he had a pointed hat and a wand to go with his robe, but I'm sure he'll be a great asset to our court — especially if the electricity reservoir runs dry or we need to change any base metals into gold.

[3] Honest.

[4] I got it from Ikola. He's just gonna be handy as hell to have around.

this happen?" This, of course, is precisely the question Ms. Lane wants you to ask. On the football field of litigation, you've got a first and goal at the *res ipsa loquitur* one-yard line when people hear your facts and ask, "How could something like this happen?"

And the answer, of course, is, "Technology run amok."

First of all, we have the whole "LobsterGram" thing. I think all I need to say about this is that in 1950, when somebody showed up at the door with a "container designed to keep things cold," your first thought was not that someone had sent you frozen lobster. Therefore, if it turned out not to be expensive crustaceans, but rather the frozen leg of your deceased father, your mental anguish was not compounded by having to recalculate your dinner plans. So, at the very least, modern technology is responsible to some degree for the depth of Ms. Lane's mental anguish.

Not to mention the fact that modern technology has enabled this poor woman to live in North Pole, Alaska. This is where Santa Claus lives, with the reindeer and the elves and Mrs. Claus and no — as far as I can determine from the literature — qualified grief counselors. Had modern technology not enabled her to live in this God-forsaken outpost, she could have phoned a helpful psychologist in West Covina or Walnut Creek and mitigated her damages.

But, science having overachieved to the point where we can live in places only slightly more hospitable than a barrel of liquid nitrogen, the meter kept running on Ms. Lane's pain. Ka-ching, ka-ching.

And, of course, the real culprit is this whole DNA thing, which is what spawned this cause of action in the first place. Here's how that works. Seems Ms. Lane's father died in North Dakota and left his $200,000 estate to Ms. Lane, who was his only child, but whose mother he had never married.

Ms. Lane's aunt challenged the will because she didn't believe Ms. Lane was in fact the decedent's daughter.[5] She got a North Dakota judge to order the body exhumed and tested. This being 2003, we didn't have to settle for just comparing photographs of Ms. Lane and the putative father and inquiring whether Ms. Lane had a tendency to

---

5 - And because she didn't get diddly, and she was his sister, for crying out loud. (These are legal terms, so I didn't need Ikola's help on them.)

bloat when she ate dairy. We could do DNA testing.

Apparently Ms. Lane's father had used up most of his DNA before dying, or maybe he just didn't have much, and nobody had pulled up in a tank truck with a hose and offered to refill his DNA reservoir, because the company that ran the test wasn't able to just scrape off a couple of cells like they do on "CSI: Miami."

Instead, they needed an entire drumstick. They had to saw off part of dad's leg.

At this point, the Reuters story gets a little hard to sort out. Carolyn Caskey, the president of Identigene[6], the Houston company that did the sawing and examining, says, "We have a court order that says send it to this place and this woman; I feel like I'm in the Twilight Zone."[7]

The North Dakota judge who allegedly ordered the leg of dad sent to Ms. Lane is not quoted in the story. I'm betting his position is gonna be, "The results, you dipstick; I said send her the results, not the leg."

I have to admit to a set of biases here. I'm generally pro-judge and anti-sending-legs-through-the-mail, so maybe I can't claim objectivity. But I kinda feel like maybe if you get a court order that seems to require you to send body parts to somebody not known by you to be in the habit of generally receiving body parts, you might want to seek clarification.

Fortunately, I don't have to sort this one out. Which is good, because I wouldn't have a clue where to start. Can you get mental anguish damages for this sort of breach of contract? If so, how much is the mental anguish of having a blood relative's body part mailed to you worth? How much is the pain of NOT getting a free lobster dinner after getting your stomach all set for it worth? How reasonable is

---

6 - And, at the risk of beating a dead horse, let me point out that there were no companies called "Identigene" when I was being steered to law school. I think if you get flesh and blood of your own flesh and blood from a company called Identigene, you have to expect Luddites like me to nod knowingly and say, "I told you modern technology was out of control."

7 - I've been to Houston: She's on firm footing with the "Twilight Zone" simile.

it to rely on an order from anyone who has chosen to live in North Dakota? These are all questions that would bring my poor little mind boggling to a screeching — not to mention shouting, cursing and breaking furniture — halt.

But, as long as modern technology allows people to live in otherwise uninhabitable places like North Pole and North Dakota and Houston, and can figure out whether they're left-handed, Lebanese or limacine by analyzing their saliva, we're gonna have to deal with more and more of these cases. We had better get used to them.

Especially since modern technology seems to have made some major breakthroughs in other areas. I read today that, "A federal judge on Thursday sentenced a man to two years in prison for a multimillion-dollar scam involving McDonald's promotional games such as 'Monopoly' and 'Who Wants to Be a Millionaire.' " According to the Associated Press, "Jerome Pearl, 45, of Miami, also must pay restitution of $786,500 at $50 a month."

This may be bad news to Mr. Pearl, but on behalf of the rest of humanity, I am absolutely thrilled that we've apparently overcome this limited life-span thing that has been dogging humanity lo these many years. Even assuming the court's order were — for some reason — interest-free, Ray Ikola tells me Mr. Pearl would have to live to the ripe old age of 15,775 to pay off this judgment.

I figure with that kind of time — assuming I can keep people from sawing off my legs and mailing them to my daughters — I can figure out PowerPoint. ❖

— January 2003

A Good Walk Improved

Getting a grip on the newest development in Southern California criminal law

Ogden Nash once said, "Middle age is when you're sitting at home on Saturday night and the telephone rings and you hope it isn't for you." Bedsworth's Corollary to Nash's Law states that, "Old age is when you're sitting at home on Saturday night and the telephone rings and you don't care if it's for you or not because you aren't answering anyway."

I think I have officially reached that latter stage. I have become so frightened by my own inability to understand what younger people are doing that I have decided I will no longer answer my phone unless I have a research attorney around to explain the phone call to me.

I came to this conclusion in New York. I went to Manhattan for a wedding and stayed in a friend's apartment. There my wife, Kelly, and I were treated to Manhattan-style community access television — which turned out to be much like Manhattan-style clam chowder:

so much more colorful than the original as to be unrecognizable as the same thing.

I don't know what community access TV is like in your neck of the woods. In mine, it's high school volleyball and city council meetings and interviews with local personalities[1] and Wayne's World wannabes — all of which are strangely engaging in a sadomasochistic sort of way. But in Manhattan, it is much different.

Kelly and I were treated[2] to a 20-minute videotape of a woman trying on pantyhose. That's right. She would put on a pair of pantyhose, take them off, open a new package, try them on, take them off, open a new package, try them on, *etcetera usque ad somnium.* I don't know how long this "show" lasted, because we caught it in midstream, while changing channels. But it was at least 20 minutes and a half-dozen pair of pantyhose.

To fully appreciate the entertainment value of this programming, you need to understand that the ... protagonist ... was not especially attractive, was wearing decidedly unsexy underwear, and never revealed anything more than she would have revealed at a public pool. She said not a word, except to muse upon each pair of hose before she tried it on ("Suntan beige," or "Honey nude," or — and Olivier couldn't have delivered this one better — "Taupe").

Furthermore, she did nothing remotely provocative.[3] Only when the ... presentation ... ended, and the credits appeared, along with a promo telling us we'd been watching, "New York's Number One Fetish Show," did we realize just how far we'd strayed from Kansas, Toto.

I was reminded of a friend who, years ago, fell asleep in front of public television and awoke in the middle of an episode of Monty Python's Flying Circus, which he had never before seen and was utterly incapable of imagining. He thought he'd lost his mind.

All in all, "New York's Number One Fetish Show" was one of the

---

1 - Who turn out not to have any.

2 - I use the word advisedly; you can decide for yourself whether there's any irony involved after you read the next two paragraphs.

3 - At one point, she took out a wooden ruler and rubbed it along her calves. Should that have done something for me?

most entertaining half-hours of my life. Kelly and I vacillated back and forth between hysterical laughter and absolute mystification. The vote on going to the wedding the next night or staying home and looking for another episode of the Pantyhose Lady was one-to-one.[4] But much as I enjoyed it, the inescapable fact was that I was completely out of the loop on what the cool fetishes were.

Initially, I was ready to write that off to right-coast lunacy. I had just about convinced myself that my inability to relate to this divertissement was a function not of age, but of cultural deprivation. I am, after all, nowhere near as sophisticated as folks in midtown Manhattan. I haven't had the same exposure to culture — or, in this case, subculture — they've had, and couldn't have expected to be as hip as they are, even when I was in my prime.[5] Besides, Kelly's not old, and she purported to be as bewildered by the Pantyhose Lady as I was.

But today's paper disabused me of all my defenses. Today's Los Angeles Times stripped away the last vestiges of my "cultural differences" claim and instead demonstrated my complete inability to appreciate modern vice. Today I read, "Golf Course Prostitution Raid in Norco Leads to 6 Arrests."

Here is what it said in the very first sentence of the article: "Authorities arrested six people early Saturday morning, hours after raiding a Norco golf tournament that allegedly offered romps with prostitutes inside tents set up on the greens."

Sex tents. On the greens.

Now I know I'm old. Now I know I am completely out of touch with the younger generations.[6] Here is a crime which combines my two favorite things in life, and I have never before heard of it.

And it was going on right next door. Not in Manhattan, not in Newfoundland, not on some asteroid in the outer Van Allen Belt. In Norco. You can drive from my home to Norco in 45 minutes. Less,

---

4 - Tie votes in our family are decided on a "winners' out" basis, like pick-up basketball games, and, having never previously won, I lost this one as well.

5 - Which, as I recall, was a Tuesday during the Nixon administration.

6 - Here's another clue: I can no longer refer to the "younger generation" singular. I think when you have to type "younger generations" you can pretty much say goodbye to being the target audience of the Nike ads.

if you know there's golf prostitution there.

GOLF PROSTITUTION! Where was that when I could have benefited from it? How many abysmal rounds of golf have I played that could have been immeasurably improved by the simple erection[7] of "tents set up on the green"? Now I've reached an age where "lost balls" and "two strokes a side" are terms I relate exclusively to golf, and I fear it's too late for me to adjust to the game as it's played in Norco.[8]

According to the article, "Riverside County sheriff's deputies, some of whom hid in trees to conduct surveillance," broke up the tournament that was being played and arrested three women, two golf course employees, and a prospective customer.

Picture this, if you will. The golf course is littered with tents. ON THE GREENS. There are deputy sheriffs perched in the trees. Prostitutes are plying their wares while golf carts driven by men in plaid pants whiz by. And somewhere in the midst of all this, some poor fool is shanking a six-iron into the woods and worrying that he's two shots back with four to play. This isn't a golf tournament, it's a Marx Brothers movie.

And what's the response of the golf course owner? "These are clean-cut guys, and I can tell you we had no connection whatsoever to what was going on."

Obviously, this is a man who failed Marketing 101. Here he's handed the best publicity in the history of the game — which dates back to a British Open won by a Neanderthal with three sticks and a rock — and he tries to dodge it. The Los Angeles Times wants to tell everyone within 15 zip codes of his golf course that it's the best place in the universe to play a round,[9] and he's trying to say it was a fluke. Jeez, has he no sense of public[10] relations at all!?

Let me try to help him out. This took place at Hidden Valley Golf

---

7 - You don't really think I've got the nerve to footnote this, do you? Make up your own. I shouldn't have to do all the work here.

8 - Mark Twain once called golf "a good walk, spoiled." Norco rules might have changed his mind.

9 - Or play around.

10 - [Editor: Please make sure no letters are left out of this word — Beds]

Club. The address is 10 Clubhouse Drive, Norco, Calif., 92860. And yes, that was its name before this took place.

Golfers — or aficionados of the criminal law, wishing to make a pilgrimage to the site of this historic crime — may call 909-737-1010 for tee times. Or whatever.

I've never played Hidden Valley, and now I probably never will. Kelly tells me I've lost another tie vote on whether I want to play there. Besides, I guarantee you their phones have been ringing off the hook with people who've never previously played there, but want to now.

You probably can't get a tee time until 2008. Hell, you probably can't even get a space in the parking lot until November.

The Times, which is even older than I am, finds this inexplicable. It says, "Despite the scandal, Hidden Valley wasn't hurting for golfers Saturday morning. Employees scrambled to keep up with customers streaming in the door."

"DESPITE the scandal?"

"DESPITE?!" The Los Angeles Times is surprised that the day after they revealed there were prostitutes working a local golf course, a large number of men inexplicably appeared? Quick, somebody call Woodward and Bernstein; we may want to look into this.

I dunno. The Times may find this mysterious. Me, I just find it depressing. I've learned this week that I am too superannuated to appreciate a fetish channel, I've spent my entire life playing golf courses which did not feature prostitution, and I subscribe to a newspaper which purports to be puzzled by the one thing in their entire story that seems self-evident to me.

I have little doubt that when that newspaper arrives tomorrow, it will contain even more evidence that age has overtaken me. And if the phone rings, I'm afraid it will be someone inviting me to partake in still another vice which seems to have passed me by.

About all that's left for me is the security of my daily routine: my walks, my work, an occasional trip to the market. Let's see, a dozen eggs, a quart of milk, a loaf of bread, a dozen golf balls, six pairs of pantyhose .... ❖

— July 2002

The Silly Season

Why must Californians take the initiative?

I met a woman from Connecticut at my daughter's softball game the other night. This is her first year in Southern California, and I asked her how she liked it. "It's fine," she said, without enthusiasm. "The kids love it. I miss the seasons, though."

This is, of course, a common complaint. It is usually voiced by women. Men see no problem. We have all four seasons: baseball, football, basketball and hockey. And we get the East Coast ballgames in the morning on weekends, so there's absolutely no time for yard-work — unlike our oppressed right coast brethren, who have no excuse other than the fact they were up all night watching the Mets-Giants game which didn't start until 10-freaking-30 and then went 11 innings before that idiot manager put Strabowski in to face Martinez for chrissakes! Strabowski!

Nor do I understand how anyone can miss winter. Sure, snow is lovely — if you can just sit around and look at it. Snow is delightful if you're relaxing after a day on the slopes, sipping hot chocolate and watching the kids build a snowman. But it's a huge pain in the ... back

... if you have to shovel it at 6 in the morning four days in a row so you can get the Dodge out of the garage and then slide around like mercury on a hotplate all the way to work.

People who lament our dearth of seasons are almost never talking about the joy of sleet. They rarely say they miss the 106 percent humidity, and I seldom hear them rhapsodizing about ice storms or hurricanes or floods. Apparently the hole in the ozone layer which covers this nation east of the Mississippi allows cosmic rays to damage all the seasonal parts of the brain except the part which remembers fall breezes and leaves changing color.

Besides, those of us lucky enough to have grown up out here[1] know we do have seasons, and they're easily recognizable. You know it's fall when you buy your annual issue of TV Guide: the one with all the new shows previewed. Winter begins when you have to put on a sweater to play golf. It's spring when the Angels start lying about their pitching staff. And summer is when you can't get from your car to the supermarket because of all the people pestering you to sign their initiative petitions.

Summer is my favorite. Initiative qualifying season. I just love it when I see all those card tables set up in front of Costco.

I read the petition, then I interrogate the signature-gatherers about the pros and cons. The signature-gatherers, of course, have no idea what those are. As far as they're concerned, the pros are that they're getting paid to collect signatures, and the cons are that they have to deal with people like me.

So I insist they explain the initiative to me. That's always good for a laugh.

Then, no matter what the subject matter, I tell them this is exactly what they tried in Sweden in 1972 and the result was their alcoholism rate tripled and birth defects rose by a factor of 9. Then I shout at them in a voice so loud it interferes with communications at LAX that they're just unwitting dupes of the Trilateral Commission, and none of this would be necessary if we hadn't fluoridated the orange groves. And furthermore, they should be ashamed of themselves for promoting such blatant fascism, racism, sexism, specism,

---

1- I am 52 years old. In all that time I have not yet once — not ever — had to put chains on a single tire.

Manichaeism or whatever I think will horrify them the most. Then I let them spend 20 minutes calming me down. Then, after I've wasted a half-hour of their time, I tell them they've convinced me they're absolutely right, and I wish them the best in their quest to save the universe, but I can't sign because I'm just visiting from Connecticut (you know, it gets so humid in the summer ... and the mosquitoes!) and I'm not registered here.

You can't buy that kind of entertainment.

And you can't hardly find it anywhere but California. According to The Orange County Register, there are about 40 initiatives vying for space on the November ballot. Forty![2] You just know they aren't gonna have 40 initiatives competing for signatures at the Costcos of Iowa and Alabama and Maryland. Those folks think card tables are for playing cards on.

But we know better. We know they're for gathering 419,620 signatures for a statute or 670,816 for a constitutional amendment. Think about that. A half-a-million signatures. You'd think it would be tough to get half-a-million Californians to agree on something, wouldn't you? You'd think that alone would limit the number of initiatives we'd face. But apparently Californians will sign anything to get into Costco.

I gotta buck says you can't tell me how many statewide initiatives have appeared on the California ballot since 1976. Go ahead. Do the math in your head. Hell, I don't care where you do the math. Do it in your spleen. Do it in your elbow if it makes you feel better. The result's gonna be the same. And it's gonna scare the living daylights out of you.

329.

Three hundred and twenty-blanking-nine. At a half-million signatures a pop.

Three hundred and twenty-nine times the electorate of the Bear Flag Republic[3] has been called upon to decide directly what law should apply to all 34 million or so of us. Three hundred and twenty-

---

2 - This is really good news. The 20 we had on the ballot in March didn't begin to sate my appetite for parking lot improv.

3 - Let's face it, Californians are part of the United States only in the same limited sense that the Quebecois are part of Canada and the Basques are part of Spain. The rest of the country views us as an ungovernable appendage, and so should we.

nine.[4] There are Supreme Court justices who in their entire career didn't have to decide what they wanted the law to be 329 times.

And this is not easy stuff. I had to learn about Indian gaming TWICE just to understand the March ballot, because apparently a lot had changed since I learned about it WHEN IT WAS ON THE NOVEMBER 1998 BALLOT.[5] I don't know about you, but if I'm gonna have to learn these things 329 times, I wanna be paid as a legislator.

Speaking of which, where were our legislators when these 329 issues came up?[6]

Apparently, if we want the garibaldi to be the official state marine fish, the Legislature can handle it,[7] but if we need to decide what the state will recognize as a marriage or who should get the death penalty, we're on our own.

In fairness, I think the Legislature has probably come to the conclusion that they can only come up with a finite number of bad ideas by themselves — the rest are up to us. And we certainly seem up to the task. You just know some of these things became initiatives because no one could find a legislator crazy enough to introduce them.[8]

For example, one of the groups I'll be badgering amidst the exhaust fumes this summer wants to "extend the hours that bars and stores can sell alcohol from 2 a.m. until 4 a.m." Now there's a great idea.

---

4 - And that's not counting all the alphabet measures that apply only to your own county or your own city or your own vector control district.

5 - And I didn't really have that much time to study because I was busy barricading my front door to keep out the evil forces who my neighbor told me were threatening to build three jails and an airport in my spare bedroom.

6 - I know where Dick Ackerman was. He responded to my column about the guy taking pictures up women's skirts by sending me the legislation HE introduced which made that sort of thing illegal. So I'm ready to give him a pass on the 103 initiatives we've voted on since he was elected to the Assembly. But I'm not writing notes for any other legislators until they can prove their time was equally well occupied.

7 - Government Code Section 425.6. *Hypsypops robicundus* to you, too.

8 - And some of them they couldn't introduce: We had an initiative in March whose purpose was to cancel out an initiative we'd approved earlier. The Legislature is constitutionally prohibited from being that stupid; only the voters can do that.

Lord knows we're having a terribly difficult time getting people liquored up enough to drive by 2 a.m. A couple extra hours might be just the ticket.

And, of course, if we can keep 'em in the bars until 4, we can pretty much guarantee that a great number of them will be driving to work two hours later with no sleep and an illegal blood alcohol level. That should drive the rest of us off the road[9] and more or less eliminate the need for more freeway construction.

Or maybe the idea is that if they stay in the bars until 4 a.m., they'll be too drunk to walk to their cars, much less open the doors and start the things, so they'll just pile up in harmless mounds on the sidewalks.[10] Until the bars open up again at 6 and they crawl back in. This would also eliminate the need for more freeway construction.

How did our Legislature miss this brilliant idea?

And couldn't we put the folks who will be promoting it to more productive work? Like shoveling snow? ❖

— May 2000

---

9 - Literally at first, and then figuratively.

10 - California snowdrifts.

Take the Ashes and Gub

The Winner of the Dumbest Criminal of the Year Award

T. S. Eliot said, "April is the cruelest month."[1] He explained this in terms of flowers bursting through the earth and a whole lot of other metaphorical crap that doesn't bear analysis unless you've already been determined by acclamation to be a great poet.

Hell, unless you're T. S. Eliot[2], you can't even get away with "cruelest." Everybody else has to say, "most cruel." In California, we appellate types have a government office whose whole purpose is to keep us from using words like "cruelest." It's called the Reporter of Decisions for the Supreme Court and Courts of Aal. (See, Government Code Section 68900, et seq.)

The Reporter of Decisions is a nice man named Ed Jessen, and he

---

1- "The Waste Land," 1922. I like to get the redeeming social value out of the way early.

2 - Don't get me wrong. I like Eliot. I once memorized the first 64 lines of "The Love Song of J. Alfred Prufrock." I just happen to think there are parts of "The Waste Land" that make it as aptly named as this book.

and his minions[3] edit everything written for publication by the Courts of Appeal and the Supreme Court to make sure we sound official and/or erudite.[4]

They've even compiled a book, "The California Style Manual," subtitled, "A Handbook of Legal Style for California Courts and Lawyers," in a vain effort to teach us to sound like we know what we're talking about. Obviously, Jessen's title should be "Chief Sisyphus in Charge of Getting Out of the Way of the Rock on Its Way Back Down." But they couldn't get that on the letterhead, and it caused a lot of inter-office squabbling about proper capitalization, so they just went with Reporter of Decisions.

One of the things they do is watch our language. That is why no appellate court in California has ever used the word "cruelest," except in quoting someone else. And, T. S. Eliot having inexplicably moved on to the great beyond without ever having sought a position on the Court of Appeal, we probably never will.

They've apparently assigned one really smart woman to do nothing but ride herd on me. If you know basketball, you can think of it as a box-and-one defense: The rest of the team guards everyone else and Brenda Cox just follows me around.[5]

A few years ago, I had to fight like a drunken bobcat to get the Reporter of Decisions to let me use "lumberjacking" as a noun.[6] I can't imagine the brouhaha if I'd tried to use "cruelest."

But I digress. At least I think I do. I'm not even sure of that. If "digressing" is defined as "turning aside from the main subject in writing or speaking,"[7] then I have failed to digress because I have failed to establish a main subject. I wandered off course somewhere around the fifth word of the essay, well before I got to my main subject.

---

3 - Say what you will about Ed, he is a man of many minions.

4 - Imagine their despair when I was appointed.

5 - Rumor has it the Supreme Court is considering the institution of a similar system.

6 - Only me and a drunken bobcat would have cared.

7 - Which is exactly what it's defined as in The American Heritage Dictionary, and professional dictionary writers are almost as authoritative as the California Reporter's Office.

I have therefore "gressed" before I ever got to my topic. I have "pregressed." This is something that, judging by the lack of any term for it in my dictionary, has never previously happened. Congratulations on having been here to see history made.

Now I have to make sure the word gets into circulation. To that end, the word "pregressed" will be in my next six opinions, and when the Reporter of Decisions insists I replace it with an "accepted" verb, I'll offer them "lumberjacked," which has, after all, been accepted ever since *People v. Foranyic,* (1999) 64 Cal.App.4th 186, 189, when they decided I was more trouble than I was worth and let me have my way. Could someone please drop by Jessen's San Francisco office and take away any sharp objects he may have?

And now, pregression aside, it's time to actually get to where I tried to go 500 words ago, before I was so rudely interrupted by my own incapacity for linear thought, to wit: April may well be the cruelest month, but January is the month in which I always give my award for the dumbest crime of the preceding year.

I know most of these "retrospective best" awards are given in late December, but I have a day job, and it's hard to find the time to squeeze in these really important awards what with all the writs and things. So my award always comes out late. That's just the way it is. Get over it.

This year's winner was actually committed in August. The crime, that is, not the accused criminal, although he should have been committed shortly thereafter.

According to the San Francisco Chronicle, "A San Mateo man has pleaded not guilty to charges that he tried to collect a $1,500 ransom for the return of the cremated remains of a dog belonging to a Foster City family."

Wow.

That's a prize winner. I probably should have just stopped the contest right then and awarded the medal. But between this guy and the guy with the monkeys in his pants (see page 143) and all the corporate CEOs auditioning for The Gang That Couldn't Shoot Straight, I figured it was a banner year: Who knew what might be done before New Year's?

But dead-dog extortion is pretty hard to top. So our winner is Kenneth So, 23.

Technically, I may be a little premature in announcing Mr. So as this year's winner since I don't know if he's changed his plea to guilty yet. But I'm sure this is just a formality — like cashing in the winning lotto ticket — because this is a chance at immortality. Even if they've got the wrong man, I'm sure So will plead out, just to assure his place in the history of crime.

Not to mention his place in the history of words. The Chronicle's account of this story says, "The dog's cremains — as cremated remains are called — haven't been recovered."

Cremains? Cremated remains are called "cremains?" By whom? Since when?

I hope Mr. So doesn't end up in prison, because I'm pretty sure if Bubba asks you what you're in for and you indicate you were holding cremains for ransom, you'll get beat up. My experience with cons is they don't like being made fun of, and you start throwing around words like "cremains," you better have a shiv or Ed Jessen with you.

But now I am digressing. According to the Chron, So lives in San Mateo. This is good, since it marks the return of the award to California after a two-year hiatus in Arizona.[8] This is, after all, where the award belongs. If, as I am beginning to believe, Arizona is a cathedral to goofiness, California is still its Lourdes.

And what better proof of this than the allegation that Mr. So,[9] after making off with $12,000 in computers and electronic equipment, sent the homeowners a ransom note demanding $1,500 for the ashes of little Sparky.

I mean, think about it. You've just picked up $12,000 worth of modern technology for no more effort than opening an unattended sliding glass door, unplugging all the loot, and loading it into your trunk. You're sitting on your arse, sipping a cold one, trying to decide which of the swag to sell and which to plug into your own wall. But instead of dropping to your knees and thanking a merciful God that you can make a living this way, you decide to try to squeeze another

---

8 - The man who stole the mayonnaise out of the hotel refrigerator because he thought it was "community property," and the lady who assaulted her neighbor with a peanut butter sandwich.

9 - Or the unnamed someone for whom Mr. So will take the rap, in exchange for his place alongside John Dillinger, Willie Sutton and Maury Wills in the pantheon of inspired thievery.

$1,500 out of this turnip.

So you send a ransom note to the owners, telling them to meet you at the corner of Edgewater and East Hillsdale Boulevards in Foster City at 3 p.m. the next day, or they'll never see little Sparky alive again.

Oops. That's not right. Sparky's already dead.

"Bring the money to Edgewater and East Hillsdale at 3 o'clock tomorrow, or I'll incinerate your dog." No, that doesn't work either.

"If you ever want to see Sparky's urn again ..." Aw shit.

This should have been a tip-off. Remember the scene in "Take the Money and Run" where the bank robber hands the teller a note and the teller misreads it as "I have a gub," and then gets into an argument with the robber about whether he has a "gub" or a "gun"? Woody Allen's Third Rule of Criminal Endeavor: If it won't write, it ain't right.[10]

If you can't phrase the ransom note so it sounds like you've got something worth buying back, you're just not cut out for extortion.

Consider a career on the appellate bench. Or with the Reporter of Decisions. ❖

— January 2003

---

10 - Which, coincidentally, is also the Third Rule of Appellate Opinion Writing.

Why *Not* Me, Lord?

It seems that, once again, Waukegan gets all the really juicy cases

Art Hoppe, the late, much-lamented San Francisco Chronicle columnist whose bust occupies a place of prominence in my pantheon of heroes, once described the way he wrote his column. He said, "I sit down every morning and read the paper, looking for things I don't understand. And when I find one, I write a column explaining it."

I don't have anything like Hoppe's talent, so my approach is a little different. I sit down and read the paper, looking for things I don't understand; but then, instead of trying to explain them, I just write a column lamenting their incomprehensibility. This is much easier than Hoppe's approach, especially since there's so much in the world I will never understand.

Take, for example, this article from The Recorder. It says, "In a case pending in a state court in Illinois, Anna Navarrette, 21, who holds the Miss Nude Spain title, is suing Samaka Sautner, 28, her Venezuelan counterpart, over the alleged theft of a Spanish-styled, ruffled-and-sequined dress that Navarrette designed and paid to have made, according to the Waukegan Sun."

Now, living in Southern California, I am used to not understanding things printed in The Recorder. I have about as much chance of understanding what goes on in Northern California as a lobster has of understanding the infield fly rule. But even by Recorder standards, there's a whole lot not to understand about this story.

Why, for example, is a newspaper in Waukegan, Ill., called the Sun? Waukegan is at the northern edge of Illinois — due west of Detroit. Waukegan is a very northern place. You lose your concentration parking your car, you can end up in Wisconsin.

Waukegan's big tourist event is the Sleet Festival — held every year from Sept. 9 through Aug. 30. They get sunshine about as often as they get kappa rays from the planet Zantar. Jupiter's moons are warmer than Waukegan. Why in the world would they have a newspaper called the Sun?

And why in any world would they host a lawsuit between Miss Nude Spain and Miss Nude Venezuela? Under what bizarre, Kafkaesque notion of vicinage does a lawsuit between a Spaniard and a Venezuelan end up in Waukegan, Ill.?

My first thought was diversity jurisdiction. (Actually, my first thought was that The Recorder had inexplicably taken to reprinting portions of Kurt Vonnegut novels as news reports, but my second thought was diversity jurisdiction.) Problem is, the thing's in state court. I can certainly imagine a federal judge hijacking this case into his courtroom, but we state court types are usually a lot more circumspect than that.

So my instinct would be that Miss Nude Spain, not wanting to sue Miss Nude Venezuela on her home turf — where she's probably pretty popular[1] — somehow found out that Miss Nude Venezuela was doing business in Illinois.[2] I have no idea what business a Miss Nude Venezuela might do in Illinois, but I have visions of the process server walking into "Samaka's Nude Food" or "Miss Nude Venezuela's Waukegan House of Tandoori Chicken" or "Almost-Wisconsin Naked Dry Cleaning" or whatever it was, throwing down the gauntlet — and the summons — and announcing, "See you in court," with a whole new kinda gleam in his eye.

The only other thing I can think of is that they bid on it. Like the Olympics. You think maybe the city fathers of Waukegan[3] went all over the world bribing people so they could get this trial for their city? Probably not. Not unless Waukegan is governed entirely by bachelors.

So I think we're pretty much stuck with the idea that Miss Nude Venezuela was doing business in Illinois, and Miss Nude Spain chose Waukegan on the theory that they'd probably never seen a naked person there so the "Miss Nude" thing would likely go right over their heads.

But I still don't understand the gravamen of the lawsuit. We've got two national Miss Nudes here, arguing over a dress. This is like Steve Forbes and George W. Bush arguing over an autographed picture of FDR. I mean, if you're the best-looking naked woman in Spain, what do you care if somebody's got one of your dresses in Venezuela? Much less Waukegan.

But it may make more sense than would seem, at first blush[4], to be the case. The article provides a clue: It says, "The red-and-black dress is actually four separate pieces of material that can be disassembled during a stage performance."

"Disassembled." "During a stage performance." I think we have

---

1 - Actually, I'm thinking Miss Nude Venezuela is going to be pretty popular almost anywhere, but I don't think I'm supposed to say that in print.

2 - How ironic it would be if a lawsuit between Miss Nude Venezuela and Miss Nude Spain should rely upon *International Shoe* to establish jurisdiction.

3 - No, this is not a thoughtless sexism. I just doubt very much that the city mothers wanted anything to do with this case.

4 - A phrase which may never previously have been used with regard to a Miss Nude pageant.

women in Orange County who "disassemble" their clothing during "stage performances." I think I wrote about that in *Tily B. Inc. v. City of Newport Beach*, 69 Cal.App.4th 1. This could come as disquieting news to the people of Waukegan.

But it does shed some light on my next question, which is, just how does someone become Miss Nude Spain? I'm pretty sure I understand how you win the World Cup or get appointed to the Franchise Tax Board or become a priest. Until this, though, I would not have had a clue how you got to be Miss Nude Spain.[5] Evidently, there's a considerable amount of showwomanship[6] involved. And, oxymoronic as it may seem, you apparently can't become Miss Nude World without the right costume. To disassemble.

This might explain the fact that the most famous Miss Nude is someone named Holly Montana, who was a Miss Nude Universe. I assume this is a more prestigious title than Miss Nude World, requiring, as it must, that a contestant defeat not only earthlings, but Klingons and Ewoks as well.

I don't know much about Miss Montana.[7] There were several Web sites which suggested themselves as sites for research about her, but they all had the look of places which would be hard for me to explain to the Commission on Judicial Performance, so I just gleaned what I could from the blurbs describing them and moved on. But, as I say, Miss Montana seems to have been the Michael Jordan of this kind of competition.

And it appears that you can't just walk out on the runway nude and expect to win. Apparently the title should be "Miss-Started-Out-Clothed-and-Then-Became-Nude-Probably-Rather-Suggestively-Spain." And for that you need a good "Started-Out-Clothed" outfit.

According to Miss Nude Spain's lawyer[8], she loaned this particular "Started-Out-Clothed" outfit to Miss Nude Venezuela last July, but in October they had a falling-out and she refused to give it back. Miss Nude Venezuela's lawyer counters that the "falling-out"[9]

5 - Other, that is, than being a woman and being naked. In Spain.

6 - I know it's not a word, but it's a whole lot easier than fielding nasty letters about "showmanship" being sexist.

7 - Which, I reiterate, is a name rather than a title.

8 - Now there's a client to feature in your firm resume.

9 - Strikes me as a strikingly inapt term for a discussion about clothing designed to be disassembled on a runway, but it's the one they chose.

consisted of Miss Nude Venezuela finishing higher in the Miss Nude World Pageant than Miss Nude Spain. He suggests it has nothing to do with the dress per se, but is more about bruised ego. He's cross-complaining for the cost of "storing the dress," apparently with a straight face.

I mean, can you imagine the cross-complaint: "Defendant/Cross-complainant seeks damages in the amount of four dollars as the rental value of the box in which said dress has been stored for the last 93 days"? Whoa, this one's going straight to the complex litigation panel. Somebody call Erwin Chemerinsky; we're gonna need some high-powered help on this.

Which brings me to my last question: Why don't I ever get cases like this? I mean, I just know they're gonna have to see the dress demonstrated in order to compute the damages.[10] I could have handled that. In my whole career I've never had so much as a Nude Miss East Garden Grove appear before me.

I thought *Tily B., supra*, was gonna be that kind of case. It was all about nude dancing. I couldn't wait to start researching it. But my colleagues insisted it turned on all kinds of arcane constitutional desiderata and flatly vetoed my suggestion that we had to view the scene. Memo to Supreme Court: If we got that one wrong, it wasn't my fault. It was Sills and Crosby's absurdly narrow view of what constituted the appellate record.

Anyway, some guy named Michael Fritz of the Lake County Illinois Circuit Court gets to hear this case. I'm just sure he won't appreciate it as much as I would have.

But he'll probably understand it better. ❖

— April 2002

---

10 - Yeah, I know it's a nonsequitur, but I betcha it's as good as whatever reason the Waukegan judge comes up with.

Clueless in Columbus

We give Midwesterners way too much credit

I've always had a warm spot in my heart for Ohio. It was, after all, the first state whose name I could spell, and — really — you never forget your first. Besides, like most of us here on the left coast, I've spent my whole life hearing how wise and sensible and "down-to-earth" folks in the Midwest are. "Sturdy pioneer stock." "Rock solid values." "America's heartland."

I've been brainwashed into thinking people are somehow more likely to be rational and level-headed if they grew up where weather can kill you[1] and you're surrounded entirely by people who know what "shoats" and "gilts" are.

Most of this rubbish is doled out by people who either live in the Midwest or *used* to live in the Midwest. As near as I can determine, 50 percent of Southern California is populated by descendants of

---

1- "Poor Cousin Earl. You know, he was never the same after he got caught in that hailstorm without his hat. So I guess the fact he wandered out into the tornado shouldn't surprise us any."

Tom Joad, Laura Ingalls Wilder, William Howard Taft and Lassie. And another 25 percent are people who watched last year's Rose Bowl game after shoveling a foot of snow off their driveway and decided midway through the third quarter — when it started to snow ... again — that Jed Clampett was right: "Californy, that's the place ya gotta be."

Now, I'm generally willing to cut them some slack. They have, after all, lived a hard life, for the most part. If you spend the freezing winter bundled up in 85 pounds of clothing and the sweltering summer carrying around 8 ounces of clothing soaked in 84 pounds of sweat, I figure you deserve a little leeway.

But I must admit to having a difficult time refraining from asking them, "If it's so great in the Midwest, how come all the Midwesterners I know live in Mid-West Covina?" I mean, I just assumed they moved out here to escape a region in which Bobby Knight, George Halas and Mayor Daley could be cultural icons. Lord knows I would have.

Near as I can determine, if you live in a state where you can drive due north and eventually hit a Great Lake, you're probably goofy as a June bug. So if I ever needed to sell a product, I'd want to hire the ad agency that came up with that "steady, dependable, practical Midwesterner" crock.

I mention this now because my morning paper tells me that Mayor Richard M. Daley[2] and a city of Chicago construction crew went out to Chicago's largest general aviation airport at 1:30 in the morning two nights ago, and tore up the runway. The mayor explained that he was concerned that the airport was pretty close to Chicago's very tall buildings, and that constituted a security risk. So he gathered up some cops and some hard hats and some heavy equipment, and they went out and destroyed the place.

Now I don't know whether this is a good idea or a bad one.[3] I kinda think turning general aviation airports into concrete jumbles because of Sept. 11 is a rather Luddite response to the problem. And the fact it took the mayor a year and a half to think of this measure — a measure that NO ONE ELSE IN AMERICA HAD PREVIOUSLY

---

2 - Pliny the Younger.

3 - If you're a regular reader, you know just how limited my ability to distinguish good ideas from bad ones is.

SUGGESTED — might have indicated to him that maybe it needed a little more thinking through.

But what concerns me more is the fact that while Chicago has 50 aldermen and a council system designed to make decisions for the city, exactly — and literally — none of them was consulted about this. And the action was taken at 1:30 in the morning.

I don't know. I guess it's different in the Midwest, but out here in America's Loony Bin, those two factors — completely bypassing the body entrusted with such decisions and acting at an hour when the only observers would be the guys driving the Entenmann's trucks — would be considered *prima facie* evidence of both the existence of a conspiracy and the need to appoint a conservator.

I mean, what would be your response if Mayor Willie Brown drove out to Treasure Island at midnight tonight and blew up the Bay Bridge, explaining that he did so because that was the primary avenue into San Francisco for terrorists?[4]

And Mayor Daley's explanation was classic: He said he acted without consulting the City Council "to avoid a lot of contentiousness." Well, I say "Amen" to that. That damned representative government thing can be one helluva nuisance. Thank God for the cover of darkness.

Now, in the words of one of the great San Franciscans, "I know what you're thinkin'." You're thinking this is one isolated instance involving one … unusual … city official.

OK then, let's talk about Ohio. You'll recall I started out talking about Ohio and then got distracted by nocturnal airport eradication — a concept I had not hitherto encountered. But now I'm ready to get back on track — assuming Mayor Daley hasn't blown it up.

Ohio has a supreme court, which decided a couple of months ago to reduce a punitive damages award from $49 million to $30 million. No problem there. State supreme courts do that all the time. I'm pretty sure it's in the job description: right next to supermarket ribbon cuttings and graduation speeches.

But then they went a little further. They ordered that most of the damages should be diverted away from the plaintiff. All right, that's a little more "out there," but several states have done that — order-

---

4 - Note to editor: Please make sure this hasn't actually happened before running this piece.

ing that the funds go into the state general fund or an enumerated special fund.[5]

But I'm not aware of any previous court that has ordered that the money go into its *own* charity, which it *created* in the opinion.

That's right. You must have read about this. It made all the newspapers in California, even if it seemed unremarkable to the folks living between the Rockies and the Alleghenies.[6]

They ordered that $20 million go into a fund they named "the Esther Dardinger Fund — in honor of the plaintiff's deceased wife — at the James Cancer Hospital and Solove Research Institute at the Ohio State University in Columbus." At least they didn't name it after themselves.

But it puts a lot of pressure on the rest of us appellate types. I'm sure the California Supreme Court's phones have been ringing off the hook with calls from the justices' alma maters, wanting a few mil diverted into their research programs. One of my colleagues suggested we should divert a few punies into the football program at his school, which hasn't played in the Rose Bowl since the first Mayor Daley was in office.

But — call me hidebound and antiquated — I think this is precisely the kind of bad idea California usually gets blamed for. And, unlike jurists in other states, who could point at us if we did something this spectacularly ditzy, and say, "Hey, it's California; what did you expect?" we have to deal with the perception of our constituents that this is a "level-headed, solid, trustworthy Midwest" idea.

Everybody out here thinks if they're doing it in Ohio, it must be solid as savings bonds. They'll probably be amazed when I tell them about the Fourth Ohio District Court of Appeals' decision that — so help me, I'm not making this up — "A man was exercising his free speech rights when he barked back at a police dog."

Honest. That's what it says right here in my local legal newspaper.

---

5 - As far as I know, the states that have acted in this way have done so through their LEGISLATURES, rather than through seven jurists, but let's not get hung up on technicalities here. Surely we've learned *something* from Mayor Daley.

6 - In fairness, I have to admit *some* heartlanders commented on this action. Professor Richard A. Epstein of the University of Chicago Law School called it "grotesque." Must not be native to the area.

Barking at a police dog is free speech, and one Jeremy Gilchrist's conviction for "taunting or tormenting a police dog or horse" has been reversed on the grounds it violated the First Amendment.

Once again, I must confess my ignorance. I only read the Federalist Papers once. I probably just missed the part about free speech including barking like a dog. I assume that right is found in the same constitutional penumbra that protects yodeling during symphonies and the noise my 10-year-old nephew makes with his hand in his armpit.

But if barking like a dog is protected by the First Amendment, how can we call the police when our neighbor's dog does it at 2 a.m.?[7] Surely we're not so specist as to deny to dogs the right we so jealously guard for humans. Surely a bad imitation of Fido isn't entitled to more protection than the original.

And how do we know these aren't fighting words that are being barked? Free speech doesn't protect fighting words. How do we know Jeremy Gilchrist didn't bark something at the police dog that was "inherently likely to provoke an immediate violent reaction?" [8] Wouldn't you just love to read an opinion that actually addressed whose burden it was to prove whether the barking included "words" that would not merit constitutional protection under *Cohen v. California,* (1971) 403 U.S. 15.

And doesn't the Ohio court's ruling open up the rather difficult question of whether a First Amendment defense can include the claim that even if the barking did include fighting words, they were true? Almost 20 years ago, in *In re John V.,* 167 Cal.App.3d 761, the Fourth District Court of Appeal *in California* held that John V.'s act of calling his neighbor a "fucking bitch" constituted the utterance of "fighting words" and was punishable under Penal Code Section 415, without offending the First Amendment.

But try to apply that holding to the Ohio case. What if Gilchrist was barking "fucking bitch" at the police dog? Are those fighting words or an accurate assessment of the dog?

7 - Probably in response to Daley Deconstruction Associates working in the neighborhood.

8 - This is the wording of California Penal Code Section 415(3), usually referred to as "disturbing the peace," which has been held to pass First Amendment muster.

The dog's name was "Pepsie." For all I know, she was exactly what John V. called his neighbor. Does that change the First Amendment analysis? In other words, to express the issue in a sentence that should embarrass the living daylights out of any 21st century system of justice, "Can you be prosecuted for barking fighting words if they're true?"

I don't know. I'll probably have to read the Ohio decision to get a handle on the proper analysis of freedom of bark issues.

And even then I'll be laboring under a handicap. I'm a native Californian. I took both my degrees here. I am wholly unprepared to deal with Midwestern issues. My head is just not sufficiently flat. I mean, level. ❖

— May 2003

We, the People of the State of ... Mmm ... Uh ...

The case of the purloined preamble

Horace Walpole was a minor English author of the mid-18th century. He wrote the first Gothic novel, "The Castle of Otranto," a fact whose memorization in college used up hundreds of valuable brain cells I didn't really have to spare, and whose total value to me in my entire life up to now has been one point on a 20-point quiz that was probably 1 percent of a grade in a class I didn't need to graduate.

Unfortunately, I find you don't get to choose what you remember in life. Some brain cells are apparently unexpungible, and if you fill them with Nellie Fox's lifetime batting average or a recipe for beer bread, that's all they'll ever hold. I'm stuck with Walpole forever because of one moment of profligate memorization when I was 19.[1] Life is unfair.

Walpole said one thing that I remember. He said, "Mystery is the wisdom of blockheads." I have no clue what he intended to convey by that statement. It makes not a whit of sense to me now. But when

---

1- And Nellie Fox's lifetime batting average was .288. Profit from my example: Be careful what you stick in your head.

I was 19, I thought it was pretty cool to be able to make classical allusions to "blockheads," and now, decades later, it's apparently lodged in my gray matter like some annoying literary piece of chicken stuck between my cerebral teeth.[2]

It comes to mind now because I've come across another of life's little mysteries, and I'm convinced it involves blockheads.

Remember that little tirade I got off into last month about the Midwest? Remember how upset I was that folks in the heartland somehow got a pass on all the stupid stuff they did, while we out here on the left coast got tarred with the brush of endemic lunacy?

Well, it turns out I'm not done yet. I was so busy lambasting Ohio and Illinois, I somehow overlooked Indiana. That's not easily done, since it sits right between the other two[3] and is apparently every bit as goofy.[4]

I base this canard on an article from the South Bend Tribune, which notes that, "A portion of the state constitution displayed in a government building in Indiana isn't Indiana's after all." It's Tennessee's.

"How," you might ask, "could such a thing happen?" "How could Indiana's constitution — better yet, a portion of Indiana's constitution — become conflated with Tennessee's in a public building in Indiana?" You might ask that. Please ask that. Because I'm dying to tell you.

The short answer is, "It's a mystery." And I'm convinced it has something to do with "the wisdom of blockheads."

Seems Elkhart County, Ind., had a monument to the Ten Commandments in front of its City Hall. The ACLU, as they are wont to do, tattled to the Seventh Circuit U.S. Court of Appeals, which ordered Elkhart County to remove the monument unless the Seventh Circuit was struck by lightning within 30 days. God did not rise to the bait and Elkhart had to remove its monument and pay $63,000 in

---

2 - Yeah, I have a little trouble with the "cerebral teeth" image myself, but I'd already wasted too much time on it to rewrite the sentence. Cut me a little slack here; I've got a day job, you know.

3 - A.k.a., Moe and Curly.

4 - Although now that Bobby Knight has taken up residence in that other bastion of common sense — Texas — Indiana's goofiness is at least several decibels quieter.

legal fees.

This annoyed Bob Weaver. Actually, it probably annoyed lots of people; these church/state things usually do. And even though this case established rather conclusively that Elkhart County lawyers do not inflate their fees (in California, the attorney would have submitted a bill for $8,164,297.66 plus parts and labor), I suspect there was plenty of annoyance to go around.

But Bob is from Shipshewana. I know this because another article I found, in the University of Indiana student newspaper, says, "Weaver is from Shipshewana."[5]

Being from Shipshewana means living in a perpetual state of surliness. Every Christmas you have to write, "Shipshewana, IN 46565" on every one of your Christmas cards. Your children begin the SAT test three questions behind everybody else because they have to write out the name of the town. And when you cheer the school spellout at the high school football games, it takes the entire first half to finish, and the students lose their place halfway through, and by the time you're done only the school spelling bee champion and Bob Weaver are still cheering.

So people from Shipshewana are just generally in no mood to be trifled with.

And Bob Weaver is no exception. He was not about to be pushed around by what he regarded as lesser deities than the One-Generally-Credited-With-Having-Authored-the-Ten-Commandments.[6]

He decided to outflank the Seventh Circuit. He sold the Elkhart County commissioners on the idea of putting on display in the Elkhart County Administration Building a collection of historical documents. This collection would include the Preamble to the U.S. Constitution, the National Motto, the text of the National Anthem, Lady Justice[7], the Declaration of Independence, the Mayflower

---

5 - I don't usually read the University of Indiana student newspaper, but it's hard to pass over an article whose headline proclaims, "Man wants Commandments Commandments displayed in Elkhart County offices." I read it just to find out what "Commandments Commandments" might be. I concluded they might be a typo.

6 - This, I'm told, is the presently accepted translation of the Hebrew word, "Yah-weh."

7 - Apparently, the word "documents" is not strictly construed in Indiana.

Compact, the Bill of Rights, the Magna Carta, the Indiana State Constitution, the flag of the United States, the Indiana state flag ... and the Ten Commandments.

So on March 17, Elkhart County installed its display. And, about an hour and a half later, the Indiana Civil Liberties Union sued them again. Then Liberty Counsel, "a civil liberties legal defense and education organization," took up the cudgel for Elkhart County, and the issue was joined.

The ICLU's plaintiff complained that he was being "forced to come into direct and unwelcome contact with the Ten Commandments" — a feeling familiar to all of us who have not led perfect lives — and Liberty Counsel countered that the plaintiff was trying to "rewrite history." Ticketron began selling tickets to the hearing for double what they got for the John Cougar Mellencamp concert. They had to distribute wristbands and limit buyers to four tickets per session.

But then somebody noticed that if you stopped looking at the Ten Commandments for a minute — which should be easy to do because just about everybody's used up a few thousand brain cells on them — you would find that another part of the exhibit was flawed: The Indiana State Constitution was wrong.

Now I don't know how big the Indiana State Constitution is. (California's was written by Stephen King, and is eight words shorter than the Bible; I suspect Indiana's is more manageable.) So I don't know just how much scrutiny is required to notice that part of it is wrong, but according to the South Bend Tribune, "The reprinted preamble in the Elkhart County Administration Building is from Tennessee's state constitution, not Indiana's. It refers to Tennesseans' 'indefeasible right to worship almighty God according to the dictates of their own conscience.'"

So, as I was trying to get you to ask about a thousand words ago, how do you suppose something like that happens? How do you somehow transpose the entire preamble of another state's constitution into your own? And what is the penalty for preamble hijacking?

I love the explanation of County Commissioner Martin McCloskey. He called it "a typographical error."

Well, of course. Happens to me all the time. I'll be typing in a citation to the California Code of Civil Procedure and I'll just slip into the New Hampshire Probate Code or the Treaty of Utrecht or the Belgian Foreign Currency Act of 1946. I tell ya, with these new-fangled computers, you take your eyes off your fingers for even a second, you can end up citing the Code of Hammurabi in an uncontested divorce.

I'm sorry, Marty. I'm having difficulty seeing this as a "typo." I think somebody had better check your copy of the Ten Commandments[8] and make sure it doesn't have a few extras thrown in, like "Thou Shalt Not Lose More Than Three Conference Games a Season," and "Thou Shalt Not Join the ICLU."

And you'd better hope the state of Tennessee doesn't sue you. I mean, I've never had occasion to do the research, but I'm pretty sure most state constitutions are copyrighted. Palming off another state's preamble as your own just doesn't sound like "fair use" to me. And I'm not sure you can get out of this one for $63,000.

On the other hand, this could really put Elkhart County on the map. After all, this has to be the first time anybody managed to offend the state of Tennessee and the ACLU with the same act. ❖

— June 2003

---

8 - Or, as they're known at the University of Indiana, the "Ten Commandments Commandments."

Divorced From Reality

Kerkorian v. Kerkorian has more quirks than an "Ally McBeal" episode

So the septuagenarian is considering wedding a 22-year-old tennis pro, and all his friends are counseling him against it. To no avail. Finally, in desperation, a friend urges him, "Kirk, consider the physical consequences. What about sex? What if the strain is just too much?" To which the elderly gentleman replies, "Hey, life is a risk: If she dies, she dies."

Old joke. One that I find increasingly funny as 70 begins to loom on my own horizon more like Catalina than Fiji. But one that is at the heart of a family law case coming soon to theaters near you.

In this case the definition of "theater" is "a building, room, or outdoor structure for the presentation of plays, films, or other dramatic performances," (American Heritage Dictionary, Third Edition, p. 1859), which should apply equally well to the Los Angeles Superior Court when the matter of *Kerkorian v. Kerkorian* is played out. This should be one very dramatic performance.

According to the Los Angeles Times, Kirk Kerkorian, the elderly gentleman described in the first paragraph, is the 46th wealthiest man this side of Alpha Centauri. Forbes estimates his fortune at $6.2 billion, which is noteworthy since, as far as I can determine, he has never played baseball for the San Francisco Giants. He is trying to sell MGM Studios because he thinks he can get $7 billion for it, and he's trying to cut back on cumbersome baubles and trinkets.

He is being sued by his ex-wife, Lisa Bonder Kerkorian, whose main complaint seems to be that he came to regard her as a cumbersome bauble and trinket. She caught him out with another woman and now she wants $320,000 a month to support their 3-year-old daughter. I'll pause here so you can get someone to perform the Heimlich maneuver on you, and then we'll work our way back to the $320,000-a-month thing.

All right, let's review. Mr. Kerkorian is now 84 years old. Mrs. Kerkorian is 36. She caught him with another woman. Right away, you know this is not your garden variety divorce case.

Then there's the little matter of child support. Here's the deal. Mr. and Mrs. Kerkorian lived together for 10 years. Blissfully. Then they got married. It lasted a month. This is, of course, what noted marital expert Hugh Hefner has been saying for years. Score one for male chauvinist boars[1] everywhere.

But this isn't a completely accurate picture. According to Mrs. Kerkorian, the relationship was foundering before the marriage.[2] And Mr. Kerkorian had resisted marriage for years. But he agreed to it when he found out she was pregnant. Like all 80-year-old men, he was thrilled at the prospect of an offspring, and agreed to marry her. I assume Strom Thurmond was the best man.

There was, however, one little proviso. She had to agree to divorce him within a month of the marriage. Sounds like a bad "Ally McBeal" episode, doesn't it? Ally McBeal, hell, it sounds like something the Brothers Grimm would have come up with if

---

1- Insert here, according to your preference, "boors" and "bores" with equal effect.

2 - This is a remarkable sentence if you really think about it. How many times do people marry after the relationship heads south? Or am I being naïve? I must admit, this whole story hovers around on the very edge of my ability to comprehend.

mescaline had been available in 18th century Germany.

Well, Mrs. Kerkorian was "heartbroken,"[3] but she figured it was the best deal she could get and it would "legitimize"[4] her six-month-old daughter,[5] so she did it. The marriage was dissolved 28 days after it was ... assembled.

She had waived spousal support. That was a condition of the marriage. She says she agreed to that condition because she "believed and hoped that Kirk's and my marriage would last,"[6] and because she was afraid Kirk wouldn't marry her if she didn't.

So that's when the child support issue came up, right? Wrong. These are rich people. The rich are different.[7] Nothing changed. The divorce had no more measurable effect than the flapping of a butterfly's wings. The erstwhile Kerkorians continued their relationship as if the divorce were nothing more than some odd little legal vaccination they were required to pick up for overseas travel.

"Their falling out, according to the court file, came during the summer of 2000 when she confronted him about rumors that he'd been seeing other women," the Times explained. "While she vacationed at a $100,000 a month Malibu beach house,[8] he traveled in Europe and sailed aboard a chartered 209-foot yacht." How can such a relationship collapse? you're asking yourself. They're half a world apart from each other making Lifestyles of the Rich and Famous look like a bad day in Appalachia.

But, unfortunately, he didn't stay on the yacht. "Finally, that Au-

---

3 - Her word.

4 - Her complaint's word.

5- I don't really understand this, since a marriage when the child is six months old hardly seems to change the fact of being "born out of wedlock," but the whole concept of illegitimacy seems so ridiculously pre-Industrial Revolution to me that I don't waste much time trying to figure it out.

6 - Last? What, beyond 28 days? How? The deal was divorce within a month. In light of this, your guess is as good as mine what these words could possibly mean.

7 - F. Scott Fitzgerald. To whom Hemingway is supposed to have retorted, "Yes, they've got more money."

8 - Now you just knew that phrase would be footnoted, didn't you? A $100,000 a month beach house. How can it cost $3,333 a day to stay anywhere whose walls are not made of chocolate?

gust, she vowed to leave Kerkorian after running into him at a Los Angeles restaurant while he was on a date with another woman." Oops.

Are you still following this? The divorced woman has now vowed to leave her ex-husband. Read this sentence closely before continuing; if your phaser isn't set to "convoluted thought," this one can get away from you.

It's just one of the annoying little chronological anomalies that will make this case very difficult for the poor peon who ends up trying to sort it out. When ordinary people run into marital difficulties, it goes something like this: 1) another woman, 2) wife leaves, 3) divorce. This one goes: 1) divorce, 2) another woman, 3) wife leaves.[9] And you thought "Memento" was confusing.

So now we get back to that $320,000 monthly child support bite. I cannot sing the long and winding road that ends up at $320,000. Too bad. It certainly seems to merit a ballad or a folk song or something. Where's the guy who wrote "The Ballad of the MTA" for the Kingston Trio? That's who should be telling this story.

But here are a few of the things I can tell you that Mrs. Kerkorian says her 3-year-old daughter, Kira,[10] needs in the way of support: First, she needs $144,000 per month for travel. That's right, one hundred and forty-four thousand dollars. American. Every month.

What, does she have warrants outstanding? The Strategic Air Command doesn't spend much more than that keeping a jet airborne 24 hours a day. On the other hand, the poor child is living in Beverly Hills; she probably needs to get out occasionally. This may seem like a lot of travel for a 3-year-old, but I guess there aren't enough Onassis or Getty or Gates scions in her immediate neighborhood.

This rather high-powered peer group would also explain the $14,000 she needs each month for parties and play dates. You go to a party for the Aga Khan's grandchild, you don't show up with a Barbie Corvette, you show up with a Corvette. A real one. You

---

9 - Yes, I know technically it's not the wife but the ex-wife who's leaving, but I really didn't think we needed technicalities in this scenario. Do you?

10 - Three. Uno, dos, tres: three. The kid is three, remember.

don't bring a GI Joe; you bring Schwarzenegger. Keeping up with the Trumps is a little tougher than keeping up with the Joneses.

According to Mrs. Kerkorian, Kira needs $4,300 a month for food plus another $5,900 for eating out. I don't know about this one. This would seem like an appropriate amount if Kira were the 83rd Airborne Division, but seems juuuuuuuuuust a little high, as Bob Uecker would say, for a 3-year-old.

Then there's $2,500 a month for "movies, theaters and outings." Come on, folks, this is the daughter of the man who owns MGM. Do you really think she's ever gonna have to pay to get into a movie in her life? And for $2,500 a month, she can pretty much buy a theater and have all her Richie Rich friends throw their parties there, thus saving a big chunk of that $144,000 per annum presently allocated to travel.

Two thousand, five hundred dollars a month is considerably more than I was given for "movies, theaters and outings," (unless you want to count the $1,500 my dad offered the garbage man to haul me away when I was 12), and — except for that unfortunate outing to see "Psycho" — my "movies, theaters and outings" experience was generally positive. I think, given the unfortunately small number of movies and plays that are really appreciable by a 3-year-old, that a smaller amount — say $2,100 a month ($70 each and every day of her life) — would probably cover it.

We're also told she needs $1,400 for laundry and cleaning. On this one I'm solidly in Mom's corner. My kids were constantly after me to provide more frequent laundering and dry cleaning of their clothes. Their therapist tells me my failure in this regard is probably what turned them into ax-murderers. Frankly, I don't see how $50 a day could possibly cover it unless little Kira is just throwing out her clothes after one wearing.[11]

And the $1,000 a month for toys, videos and books (except for the aforementioned fact that I doubt a Kerkorian heir will spend much on videos in her lifetime) seems like an absolute bargain. Most 3-year-olds have a short attention span; Kira will need a lot of toys to keep her occupied during those $144,000 worth of trips she's going to be taking.

---

[11] - Which, come to think of it, she could do for less than $1,400 a month.

But my absolute favorite is the $7,000 monthly Kira needs for charitable contributions. Charitable contributions. I don't see how I can improve on that. That simply exceeds my ability to be funny. If that doesn't make you laugh all by itself, there's nothing I can do to make it better. I would only note that this has to be good news for Toys for Tots.

So be sure to take March 11 off work so you can sit in front of Court TV and watch this one. I can't wait to see the trier of fact struggling to decide which is the real Kira: the kind little girl generous enough to spend $7,000 a month on charity, or the mean little miser who, according to her lawyer, only wants $436 a month to care for her beloved "bunny and other pets."

I know I'm anxious to get some insight into this kid. The only statement I can find attributed to her may not be very reliable. It's in the Weekly World News. They quote her as saying, "To heck with the bunny and the puppy; let them eat yachts." ❖

— January 2002

My God, You Mean There's a Sequel?

If you're tired of *Kerkorian v. Kerkorian*, just skip to the end and read the practice tip

OK, let's review. Kirk Kerkorian is an 84-year-old gazillionaire. Six months ago, I tricked you into wasting 15 precious minutes reading about his bizarre child-support dispute with Lisa Bonder. I accomplished this by printing the information in a legal newspaper rather than in the National Enquirer or the Weekly World News, where it belongs.

This, you may remember, was the column about the octogenarian whose thirty-something ex-tennis pro wife of one month (but girl-friend of 10 years) had sued for divorce — pursuant to a prenuptial promise to divorce him within a month of the marriage, one of my favorite features of the case — then lived with him for three more years until she heard he was seeing other women.

Then she sued for child support for their 4-year-old daughter in the amount of $10,667.67. Per day.

Three-hundred-twenty-thousand dollars a month to take care of little Kira.

On the off-chance that these facts aren't burned into your gray matter as indelibly as the brand of the Ponderosa, and in the equally un-likely event that you didn't spend hours trying to figure out just how you would go about spending $10,667.67 per day on a 4-year-old, I will remind you that Mr. Kerkorian contested the amount[1] and every retired judge in America except Mills Lane and William Howard Taft volunteered to handle the case.

Since that time I've been deluged with requests to update the story. All right, maybe "deluged" is too strong a word. Maybe "moistened" better describes the "flood" of phone call that poured in seeking more information about this story.

But I write a full-service column here. When I actually locate a reader, I do my level best to satisfy him. So, ... Dad, ... here's what's gone on since last we visited this story.

Ms. Bonder claimed in her lawsuit that the elderly Kerkorian was Kira's natural father, but, according to the Las Vegas Review Journal,[2] "the billionaire's lawyers said in court that he is sterile." This is, of course, always a bad break for the plaintiff in a paternity action. It's kinda like having your starting pitcher gunned down by a sniper in the first inning.

This forced Ms. Bonder to go to Plan B. She "admitted faking a DNA paternity test by using saliva she obtained from Kerkorian's adult daughter." Here I must confess to my own inadequacy in reporting this story. I have never sought another person's saliva. I've generally had plenty of my own. So I don't know just how you go about getting it. Do you just go up to the person and say, "Excuse me, I need some saliva so I can bilk your father out of the gross national product of Ecuador"?

Or do you somehow trick them into spitting: "Look that house is on fire! Let's run over there and see if we can put it out by spitting on it!" Or, "Happy Birthday! Look, I got you a spittoon; why don't you try it out!"

The need to secure an unincarcerated person's saliva never having developed in my own life, a published decision or any of the 176 episodes of "Law and Order" that have so far been "RIPPED FROM THE HEADLINES" and shown on 26 cable channels at all hours of the day and night, I have no information about how this is accomplished.

---

1 - !?.

2 - For some stories, you go to The New York Times; for some stories you go to the Las Vegas Review Journal. You don't ask Olivia Newton John to sing the blues.

But another lawsuit may contain a clue. Turns out, "real estate heir and entertainment producer Steve Bing" sued Kerkorian[3] for stealing his dental floss.

That's right, dental floss. The headline said, "Producer Sues Mogul for Dental Floss Theft."

Here's how the Daily Journal put it: "Movie producer Steve Bing has filed a $5 billion invasion-of-privacy lawsuit against MGM mogul Kirk Kerkorian. In the suit, Bing claims Kerkorian backed a scheme to steal Bing's dental floss and other items from his garbage to use in a DNA test to determine whether Bing fathered the daughter of Kerkorian's former wife."

Is there someplace where rich people go to have monopoly money issued to them? Are the damages for alleged dental floss thefts[4] paid in orange-colored $500 bills given you by someone on the other side of the kitchen table?

Five billion dollars. This is roughly what I will earn in my entire lifetime if I delay my retirement until I'm 25,053 years old.

And the gravamen of this lawsuit is that Kerkorian had a private investigator go through Bing's trash looking for dental floss so he could have it tested for DNA to show that Bing was the father of Lisa Bonder's child and HE should be paying the $320,000 a month to support her. Frankly, it seems to me that if Bing got the $5 billion he was suing for, he'd be the only person in America who could afford $320,000-a-month child support, and should be adjudged the father on that basis alone.

This, we're told, damaged Mr. Bing in the amount of three moving vans full of large bills. I don't know Mr. Bing, but if the privacy of his dental floss is worth $5 billion, I assure you I will be heeding the "no trespassing" signs at his home.

Mr. Bing — apparently no relation to Chandler Bing, but possessed of a similar sense of humor judging from this lawsuit — is a little sensitive about people getting hold of his DNA. This is because actress Elizabeth Hurley just used his DNA to prove he is the father

---

3 - Being Kerkorian's lawyer must be like having a license to print money.

4 - A phrase that sticks in the throat of this ex-prosecutor.

of her child.[5]

Ms. Hurley began seeing Bing, a 37-year-old believed to be worth about $500 million, when her relationship with actor Hugh Grant broke up. This, of course, followed Grant's well-publicized indiscretions with a Hollywood hooker who was, as I understand it, the second-cousin of Kevin Bacon's hairdresser.

Bing professed to be "astonished" when Hurley brought legal proceedings to establish his paternity. I have no idea how anybody with a net worth of $500 million can be surprised when they're sued for paternity by a woman they've had sex with who subsequently has a baby.[6] It would seem to me that such a lawsuit follows as night unto day, but Mr. Bing was "astonished" by it.

So imagine how he felt when Kerkorian started fishing around looking for floss.[7] Actually, you don't have to imagine it. I can tell you. He said in his lawsuit, "A billionaire who believes that he has enough money to take anything he wants from anyone, Kerkorian has pilfered Bing's genetic identity without his authorization." He was, in the words of Queen Victoria, "not amused."

Kerkorian's lawyer responded that Bing is the child's father (referring here to the child of Ms. Bonder, not Ms. Hurley; this stuff's more complicated than trigonometry) "and never has paid or offered to pay one dime for [her] support. ... Now, instead of doing the right thing, Mr. Bing has chosen to unleash a series of outrageously false statements to serve his own interests."

Wow. Imagine that.

This had the makings of a first-class donnybrook. I thought we might need Don King to promote it. But then Bing and Kerkorian got together and decided money is thicker than blood. The lawsuit was dropped.

According to Bing's publicist, "Kirk Kerkorian and Steve Bing jointly announced that they have amicably resolved all outstanding differences between them. They stated that the resolution came about after getting to know each other and becoming aware of additional facts that gave rise to the controversy."

5 - This gets complicated, so pay attention.

6 - Frankly, if I were Mr. Bing, I'd expect to be hit with a paternity suit if I'd had sex with a MAN. Noblesse oblige.

7 - Kerkorian apparently concluded there was a better chance of finding floss than finding condoms.

This does not augur well for Ms. Bonder. Two guys worth a couple billion, who've been arguing about who fathered your child, get together and discuss your case and end up walking away arm in arm. And to make matters worse they issue a cryptic press release regarding "additional facts that gave rise to the controversy." About the only way this could get worse would be if it turned out she'd been dating Steve Garvey.

But almost nothing in life is completely without redeeming social value[8], and this mess is no exception. There's a practice tip buried in all this "Dreck of the Rich and Famous." It's in Bing's lawsuit against Kerkorian. The Daily Journal says, "According to the suit, Bing — who describes himself as a philanthropist — will donate any winnings from the lawsuit to children's charities."

Well, now, that's how the REAL lawyers do it. They allege that if they win, they'll give the money to charity. That's brilliant.

Why haven't you thought of that? "Paragraph 62: Plaintiff, a woman motivated primarily by philanthropy and patriotism, further alleges that while the pain from her sprained elbow has been excruciating beyond the ability of words to express, and while Recalcitrant Bastards Inc., a multinational corporation whose principal place of business is in the same state as Enron, has stonewalled and lied to her at every turn, she will, nonetheless, out of the goodness of her heart, donate 90 percent of all damages over $100 million to starving children in Africa." That oughta improve your winning percentage.

And if it does, maybe you can find a few bucks to kick in for Kira Kerkorian. Poor child's probably just a step away from the soup kitchen. ❖

— September 2002

---

8 - Only child pornography and George Steinbrenner come immediately to mind.

Tomatocide and Self-Abuse (No, Not That Kind)

Discovering two new crimes just by reading the newspaper

Ambrose Bierce, whose wit and prose would have made him one of my heroes if he hadn't been such a doggedly morose s.o.b., had a great definition of imagination. I can't find it anywhere, but it was something like, "Imagination is a warehouse of facts, with a poet and a liar in joint ownership."

The liar part came to mind today when I found myself reading a newspaper article which brought home to me just how woefully ill-equipped I would have been for a life of crime. Some of these people have absolutely astonishing imaginations.

In fact, I sometimes think the thing which kept me from a life of crime was not moral fiber or economic opportunity or good role models or parental support or any of the things sociologists usually point to. It was lack of imagination. I pick up the paper some mornings and I just know I could never have thought up some of these crimes.

For example: According to The Orange County Register, "A 39-year-old Salinas woman was cited last week after trying to slay her husband's tomato plants with his .38 caliber revolver."

Honest. I don't make these things up. And I don't think the Register does either, although they need to fill a lot more space than I do.

Apparently, this lady was arguing with her husband "over the length of her hair."[1] To prove to him that her hair was the right length she blew his tomato plants to smithereens.

I find this convincing. I dare say he did, too.

But it never would have occurred to me in a gazillion years. Which, as I understand it, just happens to be the statute of limitations on vegetable crime.

Or take Christina Mack.[2] According to the Peoria Journal Star,[3] "She greased up her kitchen floor, intending to send her one-legged boyfriend tumbling to his demise. Instead, she fell and was knocked unconscious. When she came to, police charged her with attempted murder."

See, I never would have thought of that. I would have just bashed him over the head with a frozen turkey and taken my chances. Paucity of imagination.

But the criminal mind approaches even the simplest task much more analytically than I do. The criminal mind is capable of using inventiveness to solve problems I would find insurmountable.

For one thing, I wouldn't have known what to use to get the floor good and slick. All the things I spill in the kitchen seem to make the floor sticky; I would have been completely at a loss for a way to make it slippery.

Turns out the lubricant of choice is "a light household oil used for door hinges and other routine maintenance." So apparently we're talking 3-in-1 oil or that sort of thing. Canola oil and olive oil have just been done to death, and make-your-boyfriend-fall-to-his-death oil is the type of thing which a clever prosecutor can twist around in

---

1 - I'm betting he wanted it longer (most men want it longer; that's a misdemeanor). Or he said he didn't care (a lot of men don't care, but that's a felony, so they cop out to the misdemeanor of wanting it longer).

2 - You weren't really expecting to see the word "please" here, were you?

3 - For the really big stories, I need to go to the newspaper of record for the entire central Illinois heartland. Or the Weekly World News.

such a way as to make it sound pretty incriminating if it shows up on your groceries.com delivery list.

And you have to be careful where you put it. Certainly you have to be more careful than Christina was. She put it at the top of the stairs to the basement. The plan was that her 50-year-old boyfriend, Chester Parkman, who gets about on crutches, would slip at the top of the stairs and bounce down to the bottom like a slinky on coke.

It was an almost-foolproof plan. Unfortunately, Christina is not an almost-fool, she's a full-on fool. That's why she ended up a few hours later, flat on her back, looking up the nostrils of the paramedics and trying to remember what planet she was on.

Had she been able to stay out of her own oil slick, she probably could have pulled it off. A fall down the stairs could conceivably have killed Chester. And I'm sure, had he survived the fall, he never would have suspected foul play. He would, like most men, have just chalked it up to the arcane mysteries of kitchen life.

Besides, by the time he gathered his crutches and climbed back up, Christina would have mopped up the oil. She would have been standing there shaking her head disapprovingly in that way members of the superior gender have of expressing contempt while denying any such feeling. "What? All I was doing was shaking my head! I was thinking how bad I felt that you got hurt, not what a hopeless, slew-footed clod you are! I can't imagine how you could have slipped. Poor baby. Here, have a cup of oleander tea; it'll make you feel better."

And they never could have pinned anything on Christina if she'd just kept her mouth shut. True, when the police found her unconscious on the linoleum, stretched out like yesterday's yellowfin in a puddle of sewing machine oil, she'd have needed to talk fast, but I think she could have handled it.

I've had a lot of experience with police. They come across a tableau as weird as this one had to be, they'd much rather just accept your explanation than take a chance of having to do all the paperwork an attempted murder case requires.

I think she could have looked around frantically for a few seconds and then begun screaming, "My lawnmower! Where's my lawnmower? I was sitting here oiling my lawnmower when I heard a noise behind me, and next thing I knew, Officer O'Malley was asking me how many fingers I saw." I'm pretty sure they would happily have written it up as a burglary and lawnmower theft and gone on their way.

But Christina violated The First Rule of Criminal Law: "Never cop out." Also, The Second Rule of Criminal Law: "Especially, don't blab to the neighbors."

According to the Journal Star, her neighbor, Juanita Esders, said, "They were in a fight, that's all I know. She said she was going to grease up the floor so her boyfriend would fall."

Ouch. That's pretty damaging testimony. I figure Christina's toast unless she can show that Juanita and Chester had a thing going, and thereby undermine Juanita's credibility. Or maybe she could plant a little 3-in-1 oil in Juanita's apron.

But this seems unlikely, since Chester wants her back. That's right. The intended slippor[4] now insists, "I honestly think she was trying to wax the floor," which indicates to me he may previously have hit his head on the floor a few times. He says he's distraught over the prospect of losing her. He says, "She probably will come back eventually, but it's going to take some time."

Yeah, I suspect it will. Because I suspect time is what she's gonna get.

You'll be happy to hear that the local prosecutor has backed off the attempted murder charge. The Journal Star says Christina "was held Tuesday on $10,000 bond on charges of aggravated battery, attempted aggravated battery, and domestic battery."

I can understand the attempted aggravated battery charge: Had Chester been a good little victim and bounced down the stairway to heaven like he was supposed to, it would have been an aggravated battery — at least.[5] And it appears she'd taken enough steps toward the commission of that crime to go beyond mere preparation and constitute an attempt. Ergo, attempted aggravated battery.

---

4 - A word inexplicably left out of my spell-check program, but clearly more appropriate than "slipper."

5 - At least I assume it would. Incredible as it may seem to you, I know even less about Illinois law than I know about California law. I just figure by almost any definition of "aggravated battery," sending someone down a flight of stairs qualifies. Sure as hell would aggravate me.

But I must admit I'm having trouble fathoming the theory behind the charge of completed battery. As near as I can determine, Christina was the only person hurt. So if battery charges are gonna be filed, the prosecution has to come up with an absolutely miraculous theory of transferred intent. The syllogism has to set up something like, "If I'd done this and hurt you, it would have been a battery on you. Instead I did it and hurt me. Therefore it must be a battery on me."

I had some classmates in college who would have understood such logic (we won a national championship in football that year). But in almost 30 years in the criminal law, I've never heard of someone being charged with battery — or any other crime — on herself.

My understanding of the three sine qua nons of battery are (1) *actus reus,* (2) *mens rea,* and (3) *haplus schmuckus.* And I don't think it counts if (2) is in the skull — however numb — of (3).

But what do I know. Maybe Christina's on her way to Joliet[6] for battery on herself and I have just spent 1,500 words demonstrating once again the abject poverty of my imagination.

I'm lucky I've got a job where all the creative heavy lifting is done by the people at the counsel table. And their attorneys. ❖

— February 2001

---

6 - I have no idea why, but I have it in my mind there's a prison in Joliet, Ill., and I'm just way too busy to look it up. If there isn't, I'm sure somebody will tell me.

Negotiated Bliss

A million here, a million there — pretty soon you're talking a real prenuptial

I see where actors Catherine Zeta-Jones and Michael Douglas are having so much trouble working out the details of their prenuptial agreement that their wedding date is in jeopardy. As I understand it, they can't get married because they haven't yet finalized the terms of their divorce.

Yes, Virginia, the rich are different.

This kind of institutionalized pessimism isn't a problem for us peons. We tend to assume the marriage will work, at least partly because contemplating our likely assets some years down the road tends to be a little depressing.

If my wife had cared enough to haggle, she could have gotten a TV, half a computer, a complete set of Mighty Ducks drinking cups[1] and a half-interest in a six-year old Pontiac. She chose — inexplicably — to do without a prenup.

But Zeta-Jones and Douglas are $3 million apart in their negotiations. Three million a year!

According to Reuters News Service, Zeta-Jones is "distraught" because she wants $4.5 million for every year they're together be-

---

1- I had two sets.

fore the inevitable meltdown, and Douglas is only willing to give her $1.5 million a year. Another way of putting this is that she thinks living with him is going to be such a monumental pain in the arse[2] it's going to be worth $4.5 million per year, and he expects to be only $1.5 million worth of obnoxious every year.

I can see where this would be a tough call. I discussed it with my wife, Kelly, and she thinks Zeta-Jones is a little on the high side.

Kelly thinks once a man gets past 50 (Douglas is 55; I'm 52), his instinct for orneriness increases, but his ability to execute it diminishes — as does everything else except his belly — at an even greater rate. She thinks living with me is worth no more than $3.25 mil a year, and she would take that right now if she could get it.[3]

But Zeta-Jones may be looking at a little more wear-and-tear than Kelly. After all, Douglas just paid a $60 million settlement to his last wife, conceding that one of the problems with the marriage was that he is a self-confessed "sex addict."

I was going to ask Kelly how this affected her view of the fairness of the settlement, but realized it would lead me into a discussion which necessitated comparing sex with me to sex with Michael Douglas. I decided this was not a conversation I needed to have.[4]

Suffice it to say this is an issue which will doubtless eat up many, many billable hours for Michael and Catherine's lawyers, psychiatrists, aura-therapists and psychic friends.

And fast. Because, according to Reuters, "Friends of Zeta-Jones, star of such films as 'Entrapment' and 'The Mask of Zorro,' said she was distraught at the financial cloud hanging over both her wedding and the birth of her first child, due in five weeks' time." Oops. Five weeks, eh? Well, I can see where that might add to the pressure. I imagine most obstetricians advise against a lot of haggling over prenups during the last trimester of pregnancy.

In that regard, it's difficult to say whether Zeta-Jones is better or

---

2 - Since she's Welsh, I thought it appropriate to use Welsh terminology.

3 - This led to a very therapeutic discussion in which we set a mutual buy-out number of $3.2 million. First one of us who can come up with $3.2 mil can buy the other out. Since we both work for the government, I figure I can safely begin shopping for silver anniversary gifts.

4 - Even though Kelly still insists she never had sex with Michael Douglas.

worse off than Sun Bonds. Sun, you may remember, dropped by the lawyer's office on her way to the airport to fly to Las Vegas for her wedding the next day to baseball star Barry Bonds. That's when Bonds' lawyer told her "there would not be a wedding if she did not sign the premarital agreement."[5] Sun's time pressures were therefore more intense — but less permanent — than Zeta-Jones'.

Which brings us to another interesting wrinkle in the Douglas-Zeta-Jones case. The California Supreme Court is — even as we read — struggling with the significance of legal representation in these matters.[6] A divided First District Court of Appeal held that the Bonds prenup required heightened scrutiny because, *inter alia,* Sun was unrepresented. And, according to the London Sun, "While Douglas employs a team of hot-shot lawyers, Zeta-Jones … relies on her father Dai to look after her finances."

Man, oh man, the lawyers involved in this must be licking their chops. I'll bet there's saliva all over their yacht brochures. This case is a gold mine.

Not only is Zeta-Jones represented by her father, but she is a Welsh citizen living in Los Angeles, while Douglas is an American with homes in New York and Spain. Spain?! Wales?! This is the conflict-of-laws equivalent of a train wreck in a blizzard.

Can you imagine the consternation of a Welsh law firm asked to compare and contrast their case law on unrepresented prenuptial agreements entered into on foreign soil by a seriously pregnant Welsh national with the case law of Spain on the same topic? Can you imagine how unhappy they'll be that none of them knows a yacht broker?

Because once they — or their heirs and assigns (if this thing bogs down as much as I think it will[7]) — finally get some poor court somewhere on the planet to take a stab at what law to apply, they have to deal with some really difficult issues. For one thing, there's the wedding gifts.

---

5 - What a shame: I finally get around to discussing a California case with you, something from which you might actually benefit, and I find myself quoting a depublished opinion. Life is so cruel.

6 - I was going to say "affairs" but it sounded judgmental, somehow.

7 - I figure this case will be the Certified Family Law Specialist Examination until the year 2026.

Reuters says Zeta-Jones has already agreed that everything valued at more than $18,000 will be Douglas' to keep. The rest is hers. What a coincidence: I got the same deal from my wife.

But I'm a little surprised that's Douglas' deal. Re-read that paragraph. The unrepresented ingenue gets everything valued at less than $18,000 and the sleazy, grasping dirty-old-man with the "hotshot team of lawyers" gets the rest.

Michael. Buddy. Listen to me. Fire the lawyers and hire an accountant. Wedding gifts worth more than $18,000? Who's coming to this wedding — Bill Gates, Michael Jordan and Argentina?

Where do you register for $20,000 wedding gifts? What do you get for that? Six hundred Pilsner glasses? Titanium knives and forks? Is a $20,000 food processor a guy named Jacques?

This has to be a mistake, right? Nobody intentionally contracts away all the wedding gifts worth less than $18,000. So I figure the Welsh and Spanish lawyers are going to have to spend some time learning American law pertaining to capacity to contract. Somebody's bound to argue that Michael was *non compos mentis* when he made this deal. That should be good for another decade of court battles.

Not to mention the more mundane legal arithmetic. Let's suppose the Zeta-Jones-Douglases are able to agree that living together is $3 million a year worth of painful. Let's suppose they write that into their agreement. Then let's posit a marriage of 4.5 years duration. How do we split up that last $3 million for the fractional year?

Do Catherine and the baby[8] get $1.5 million? Do they get nothing unless they stick it out until the wooden anniversary date? [9]

Do we round up to five years of marriage, like the cell phone companies do minutes on your phone charges, and give them the full $3 million even though they bailed halfway through? Do we apply the sex-addiction multiplier which will doubtless be part of

---

8 - Or babies. Plural. Sex addiction is not like cocaine or compulsive gambling: It tends to add things to your life rather than subtracting them.

9 - Honest, I looked it up. The fifth anniversary is the wooden anniversary. This could complicate things even further. Given the scale on which these people operate, if Catherine stayed on until the fifth anniversary, she'd probably get a paper mill. Might be worth sticking it out that last six months if the mill had sound quarterlies.

California law by the time this case is resolved by a specially appointed Hague commission in the year 2040?

And what about the baby? Does the baby have to cut a separate
deal? If she arrives before the wedding — as presently planned —
is she entitled to a guardian *ad nuptiam* and a re-opening of the
prenup negotiations? Or does she just fall into the "gift worth more
than $18,000" category and go off to live with Douglas?

These are really difficult issues. I'm glad I don't have to deal
with them. But I feel bad knowing that somewhere, right now,
there are seven blissful little kids riding their bikes or playing soc-
cer or reading Harry Potter books oblivious to the sobering fact
that they will someday be asked by The Hague to decide this case.

And none of them will ever receive an $18,000 wedding gift. ❖

— July 2000

Gender Equality and Other Half-Baked Theories

Even coated in Teflon, men
are no match for women

I have a gender bias problem.

This is difficult to admit. Serious efforts have been made by the AOC and the CJA and CJER and several other alphabet agencies that watch over us judicial types to try to turn us into judicious types. They've spent a great deal of time and effort cleansing our brains with the most heavy-duty, industrial-strength thought soap available. And they've worked especially hard in the area of gender bias because most of us seem more capable of recognizing aliens from the planet Graustark than we are of discerning gender bias.

But I'm afraid they've failed in my case. I've kept quiet about it a long time, hoping that someone else would say what I've been thinking, and I wouldn't have to crawl out on the limb alone. No one has, so here I am ... all by myself ... saw in hand.

Men and women are not equal. We can say they are all we want, but it's not going to change anything. I've gone to all the classes. I've read all the articles. I've spent hours trying to raise my consciousness on the issue of equality of the sexes. But to no avail. I remain convinced that gender equality is a myth.

The unavoidable fact is that women are vastly superior. It's not even close.

I've known this all my life. My earliest memory of contemplating the differences between the genders dates back to fifth grade. I can remember looking around the class and concluding there was very little academic competition from members of my own gender. But Maureen McCafferty and Bernice Liebig ... they were smart. I knew I was a better kickball player, but even at age 10, I was pretty sure the course of our lives would not be determined by kickball prowess.

Which is unfortunate, because it's the last thing I can remember being a lot better at than women.

Let's face it, guys, the war's over and they won. What are the two most important things in life? Food and sex. And women control both.[1]

They're smarter than we are, prettier than we are, better organized, and a whole lot more militant. And the worst of it is they play us like we're violins with penises.

We spend our whole lives doing stuff we'd never do on our own, because some woman has somehow outmaneuvered us. We start out to eat a pizza and watch the hockey game and end up mowing the lawn and going to a charity ball. I don't think I've ever in my life looked into a champagne glass without asking myself, "How in God's name did she talk me into coming here?"

The simple fact of the matter is that if our gender were a species, it would have died out before the great auk. The only reason we're still around is that women need us to reproduce.[2]

I was painfully reminded of this dismal state of affairs last weekend. After watching my daughter throw out the potential winning run at home plate with two outs in the ninth inning, thus spectacularly eclipsing in her 12th year of life any of the athletic accomplishments of her 52-year-old father, I ventured into the kitchen to attempt a birthday cake for my wife.

I suspect I was subconsciously hoping to establish that I could compete in the kitchen as well as my daughter had competed on the diamond. I think I intended some kind of reverse-macho, in-your-

---

1 - Yeah, yeah, I know. The great chefs of the world are all men. Big deal. Try asking one of them to fix breakfast some morning.

2 - For now.

face, anything-you-can-do reassertion of male primacy. It turned out to be The Bay of Pigs with frosting. Lots of frosting.

It should have been a slam-dunk. I mean, we're talking birthday cake, here, folks. This is not particle physics. This is not even haute cuisine. Any woman with opposable thumbs could have accomplished this task.

The directions were written on a box. In English. American English. American English designed to be understood by anyone who can distinguish Huey, Dewey and Louie from giant schnauzers.

I had all the implements at hand: measuring cups, spoons, bowls, electric mixer. Of course, I had to ask my wife where they were, since I visit the cupboards where cooking utensils are kept about as often as I visit Uganda.[3]

Still, it shouldn't have been all that tough. Unlike the folks at the Jet Propulsion Laboratory, I didn't have to engage in any complex mathematical operations like converting inches into meters or anything. I just had to read and follow directions. These are skills women master[4] in the third grade, while we men are out in the neighbor's backyard kicking field goals over sawhorses and perfecting our belching technique.

They proved too much for me. After deftly spraying cake batter into three rooms with the electric mixer, I managed to turn on the oven and pour the batter into two nine-inch pans.[5]

Unfortunately, at the conclusion of the baking cycle, the cake batter chose to remain in the two nine-inch pans. I reacted like any late 20th century male: I turned the pans upside down and shook them, banged on them with a wooden spoon, and cursed them for the miserable quislings that they were. All in all, it looked pretty much like the ape creatures in the opening scene of "2001: A Space Odyssey."

My daughter explained that I had failed to spray the cake pans with something called "Pam." That's why the cake stuck to them. I informed her the cake pans were Teflon and that nothing — espe-

---

3 - And with an equivalent level of enthusiasm.

4 - Mistress?

5 - There was a short delay while I tracked down a ruler to measure the cake pan.

cially nothing as technologically pedestrian as cake — was supposed to stick to them.

Her response was eloquent beyond her years: She pointed to the cake pans and shrugged. On behalf of her gender, that shrug said, "So much for your spaceships and asteroid-blasters, Rocketboy; now, would you like me to show you where we earthling women keep the spatula?"

I was not yet defeated. One thing our culture has not failed to teach its males is the importance of saving face — especially around females. I rose to the challenge. Having coaxed one layer of the cake out of the cake pans by demonstrating my complete mastery of both spatula and vocabulary[6], I adroitly carved the less cooperative layer into precise geometric sections consisting of a half, a quarter, and several ... nuggets.[7]

Then I began the process of gluing the upper layer together with chocolate frosting. This was a task which demanded the precision and spatial savvy of an engineer and the delicate touch of a surgeon. It also demanded two cans of frosting and much more patience than my gender is capable of summoning up over anything that can't result in a double bogey.

The result was an Everest-like conquest. Also an Everest-like cake. Specifically it resembled the Lhotse face after an avalanche.

Roughly half the cake looked like a cake. The rest I like to think of as my interpretation of a cake. Kind of a baked-goods homage to Picasso.

Unfortunately, I was not able to induce my family to eat the cake until they'd stopped laughing. This almost turned it from a dessert into a breakfast.

In the meantime, I set about proving once again my complete inability to handle "woman's work." I tried to wrap my wife's birthday presents. My daughter helped. She helped by not laughing out loud during the 90 seconds it took her to wrap her gift.

But 20 minutes later, when I emerged from the bedroom, sweat-

---

6 - My college baseball coach would have been amazed; he didn't think I ever listened to him.

7 - Euclidean nuggets.

ing like I'd just run in the Belmont Stakes[8], she broke down into side-splitting guffaws. As did my wife, whose mirth was tempered only by the fact that she could see, scattered about on the floor behind me, enough crumpled and discarded wrapping material to paper the guest room.[9]

I proudly presented to my wife what I've since determined were a perfect rhomboid and an impeccable trapezoid. Perhaps her inability to appreciate anything but rectangles indicates a chink in distaff armor.

But if so, it's a painfully small one. Certainly not big enough for me to wedge my ego through.

I write this in the forlorn hope that some champion will come forth from my gender to defend us. I confess my own defeat. Maybe some guy will step forward to refute me who can repair a John Deere and scale El Capitan and captain a SWAT team.

That would be nice. Because those are all things I've read about women doing this week, and I'd like to be reassured that men can do them, too.

In the meantime, I have to go listen to a gender bias lecture. The state says we judges can have free errors and omissions insurance if we go listen to somebody tell us the genders are equal. Forget the insurance. I'm going because I want to be cheered up. ❖

— February 2000

---

8 - If I'd been a horse they would have walked me for an hour before putting me back in my stall. And the stewards would have insisted on a saliva test.

9 - It would take an accountant the better part of the day to determine whether the gifts or the wrapping materials were more costly.

"Not That I Recall"

The state of Maine takes its nudity statute quite literally

God, I love the English language. I sometimes have to remind myself of that fact when I'm parsing statutes trying to figure out what in hell the Legislature had in mind,[1] but every day I find more evidence that our mother tongue — specifically the American legislative dialect — is the single most effective engine of entertainment known to man.[2]

Take, for example, the indecent conduct law of the state of Maine. Simply put, that statute prohibits anyone from "knowingly exposing [his or her] genitals [in public] under circumstances that, in fact, are likely to cause affront or alarm."

Now this seems like a fairly simple statute. I mean, I have not a clue what that little "in fact" part is meant to accomplish, but the rest of the statute seems like something your average high school junior could figure out.

---

1 - And whether even asking that question assumes facts not in evidence.

2 - Sex comes in second, but only because dictionaries are less expensive, never want to get married and seldom give you diseases.

Certainly it seemed reasonably intelligible to the police officer in Orono, Maine, who observed Debra Ballou and Cathryn Mann running down the main street of Orono in the buff.[3] This had to be the happiest day of his career. Studies have shown that my gender expends more brain cells trying to figure out how to get college girls naked than it does trying to find food, get a job or cure cancer. And I mean expends. They die of sheer exhaustion. So to have two naked coeds suddenly appear on your radar screen, necessitating detention, arrest, transportation, booking and probably a whole lot of meaningful interrogation, has to make all those push-ups at the Police Academy look like a pretty good investment.

So the cop hits the siren[4] and pulls them over. Wouldn't you just love to know how this encounter plays itself out? Wouldn't you think any journalist worth the title would want to know what the police protocol is for dealing with young women stopped for naked running? I mean, what does the cop say? "License and registration, please?" "Can I see your ID?" "Do you know why I stopped you?" What words could you possibly speak under these circumstances without bursting into laughter?

You would think that would be a critical part of the story, wouldn't you? Yet none of the half-dozen newspaper accounts I've tracked down on this story has a word describing this part of the apprehension. I consider that a serious reporting failure; but, in fairness, the case presents no Fourth Amendment[5] or Miranda issues (*Miranda v. Arizona* (1966), 384 U.S. 436), so it's probably understandable that this deathless repartee has been lost to posterity.

Nor does the case involve any issues of intent. As a taxpayer,

---

3 - Debra and Cathryn, college juniors at the University of Maine (majoring in biology and horticultural sciences, respectively), later explained they were just trying to cheer people up, "because of the whole terrorism thing." This is probably not germane to the column, but it's so refreshing to find a story driven by women acting like idiots that I just had to include it.

4 - Honest, I'm not making this up. Debra is quoted in the Maine Campus newspaper as explaining, "We didn't see the cop sitting there and then we heard the siren." So the sirens were pulled over by a siren.

5 - Apparently no search was conducted.

you will be happy to hear that I have not checked the annotations on the Maine indecent conduct statute, but I'm pretty confident the only *mens rea* requirement is that you have a *mens*.

Actually, I guess you have to know you're naked. This is not setting the bar too high. The only person in the history of the state who might have mounted a *mens rea* defense to this statute was Sonny Liston, who, in May 1965, fought Mohammed Ali in Lewiston, Maine. Liston was knocked out by a punch that was so fast it does not show up on film. If Liston had gotten up without his trunks, he might have beaten the rap for this. Otherwise, there are no mental defenses.

Certainly an alcohol-based diminished capacity defense wasn't gonna fly. True, the girls had been drinking. As Cathryn put it, "Obviously our judgment was impaired. We probably would have stayed in our own neighborhood if we were sober." And Debra later lamented their inability to outrun the police, noting, "We'd been running and we couldn't run anymore. Next time I'd wear sneakers so I could keep running."

Both these comments indicate the girls were "impaired" at the time. Actually, they go a long way toward convincing me that they're impaired now. If they think their only mistakes were running in the wrong neighborhood and failing to accessorize, alcohol is not their only problem. But, as I explained, mental impairment — whether congenital or alcohol-induced — is not a defense.

Ballou considers the statute under which she was prosecuted a stupid law. "Clothes were invented to keep people warm and if you're not cold, you shouldn't have to wear them." Ballou, early line favorite to be elected mayor of Orono in November — whether or not she runs — thinks everyone should have the right to go naked, but she was not surprised to be arrested for it.

So, the girls were just gonna plead guilty until the arraignment judge suggested to them that they might not be covered by the statute.[6] He said the wording of the statute indicated to him that it didn't apply to them.[7] I've never met this judge, but my bet is that

---

6 - These girls never seem to be covered by anything.

7 - I'll pause here so you can go back to the second paragraph of this essay and try to figure out what the language was that concerned the judge. Hint: It was not the phrase, "in fact."

once word gets out that he's the guy who suggested the law should allow women to go around naked in public, he's never gonna have to buy another beer in his life.

Debra and Cathryn had planned on just paying the fine (indecent conduct is an "e" class misdemeanor: maximum fine, $1,000). But hearing that there was a question in one judge's mind about whether they had violated the law, they entered a plea of not guilty and went to trial.

And they won! Without a lawyer. With a defense that consisted of only one question. Ballou's cross-examination of the arresting officer was concise and to the point. She asked the state's only eyewitness, "Did you ever actually see my genitals?"

The officer's response, "Not that I recall,"[8] prompted Judge Jesse Gunther of the Third District Court in Bangor to rule that a woman naked in the street does not violate Maine law because a woman's genitals are "primarily internal" and usually not visible.

Since the statute requires that the genitals be exposed, Ballou was acquitted (the companion case against Mann was dismissed). So, as I understand it, the court's ruling was that Ballou was insulated, both from the cold and from Maine's indecent conduct law, by her pubic hair.

This has to be a first, even for American jurisprudence,[9] and it's caused something of a stir in Maine. The Orono police chief is quoted in the Bangor Daily News as worrying that, "This means that I could be at Pat's Pizza with my kids and a whole group of females could walk in unclothed and there would be no violation." (It also means people would want to buy stock in Pat's Pizza, but I think the chief was more concerned with law enforcement prob-

---

8 - I love this answer. Not that I recall??? What in hell does that mean? "I might have, but found them so unremarkable that I've forgotten?" "Perhaps, but I see so many naked women on the street it's hard to keep them straight?" What?

9 - Although, in an analogous vein, my colleagues in Division One of the Fourth District have recently decided that a man clad only in panties and bra does not violate California's indecent exposure statute. (*People v. Massicot,* 97 Cal.App.4th 920.) Like Maine, they held that "naked genitalia are required." A phrase I thought I'd never again see once I stopped receiving invitations to frat parties.

lems than with the economic health of the community.)

And the Bangor prosecutor who lost the case has admitted to being somewhat bemused by the precedent this establishes. It means the dancers at Diva's Bikini Bar in Bangor, who are prevented by city ordinance from dancing nude inside the bar, would be able to do so on the street in front of the bar. This will doubtless hurt business at Pat's Pizza, but apparently will not violate the laws of the state of Maine.

And everyone agrees that the Legislature will have to get on this right away.

Me, I'm just frustrated. No, not by the fact all the flights to Bangor seem to be booked up. Not even by the fact that women, in addition to all the other advantages they have over us poor males, get a genitalia pass in Maine. No, what bothers me is that I never get cases like this.

I mean, I know this was not the trial of the century. This was not William Jennings Bryan spouting Bible verses or Johnnie Cochran spouting Cochran verses. Nobody named Enron or Microsoft or Hewlett or Packard was involved, and there was no jury award involving more zeroes than the Japanese had at Leyte Gulf.

But *State v. Ballou* is my early season nominee for "Case I Most Wish Had Come My Way This Year." Comparative nakedness and statutory construction. Two of my favorite things.[10] ❖

— June 2002

---

10 - OK . . . One of my favorite things and one I get paid to do.

Waiter, There's a Seal Penis in My Soup!

(We figure nobody can pass up that headline)

I do not subscribe to The Wall Street Journal. I make it a rule not to read much that doesn't include pictures[1] and I don't consider an occasional line drawing of Alan Greenspan to be a picture.

Besides, the Journal generally discusses things I'm not much interested in. It has no sports page, no television listings and no comics. Reading it always makes me feel like I should put on Berlioz and some Earl Grey and find someone to discuss Proust with me. Since I don't like Proust or Berlioz or Earl Grey, I have pretty much decided to forgo the extra half-dozen IQ points the Journal would doubtless provide me and just go straight to the hockey scores.

So I am greatly beholden to Bob Mars[2] for sending me this verbatim quote from The Wall Street Journal's April 25, 2001, edition: "The vast majority of seals killed in the annual hunt are young ones with penises too small to be worth much."

---

1 - Today's practice tip for appellate lawyers.

2 - Dave Barry always refers to the nice people who send him material as "alert readers," but I know Bob Mars and he doesn't qualify for Barry's sobriquet on either ground.

I was dumbstruck by this sentence.[3]

My instincts told me I was in complete agreement with it, but I had no idea how it could possibly have come up. It was like having someone approach you on the street and ask you to sign a petition to prohibit imprisonment of marmots and chipmunks for possession of less than a gram of marjoram: You'd agree in principle, but you'd be pretty nonplussed by the suggestion some sort of action was required.

So I read The Wall Street Journal article to find out why the size of seal penises was a subject of concern to anyone but the seals. I did it at the library, so people would see me reading the paper and be reassured in the quality of their judiciary. I walked around while I read so as to get maximum exposure,[4] and I noticed a lot of people looking at me — some even pointing me out to others — and being reassured.

I do feel a lot smarter now. The Journal's prose is impeccable, its headlines restrained and tasteful, its graphs mystifying but compelling. Just paging through looking for seal penis news made me feel a lot closer to George Will.[5]

But I am less confident in my judicial abilities. The seal penis article turns out to be a terrific example of my own worst nightmare. No, not that nightmare. I haven't had that one in months. The other one: The Doctrine of Unintended Consequences.

The Doctrine of Unintended Consequences says that no matter what you do, no how you do it, no matter how thoroughly you analyze things, your actions will always have unintended consequences that outweigh their intended ones. This is every appellate justice's nightmare. We all[6] worry about writing a perfectly pedestrian, seemingly obvious opinion — resolving one single, seemingly straightforward issue — only to receive an agonized petition for rehearing and a dozen amicus briefs explaining that our opin-

---

3 - This will surprise those of you who've read my appellate opinions and just assumed this had happened decades ago.

4 - Probably the wrong word to use in a column about penises, but I have a day job: I can't be spending a lot of time on rewrite.

5 - Which my wife considers reason enough not to subscribe.

6 - Some more than others.

ion has wiped out an entire industry and will probably result in homelessness for thousands of families whose children will have to eat their pet bunnies to survive.

That's what's happened in the seal penis industry.[7] According to the Journal, there is such an industry. According to them, every year all the poor fisherman in Newfoundland "head out into the icy Atlantic to hunt seals — a dangerous job the industry is trying to bring back from decline."

It's hard to imagine an industry that consists of poor, destitute fishermen going out into icy water to risk their lives clubbing seals to death has much room to "decline." I would have a hard time deciding whether I'm more offended by the cruelty toward the seals or the cruelty toward the fishermen, but I have little trouble figuring out why this industry is in "decline."

Here is how The Wall Street Journal describes the daily routine in this line of work: "To reach their prey, the men jump out of their boats onto floating slabs of ice that can rise and fall 10 or 15 feet with the ocean swells. Leaping from slab to slab, they sometimes trek miles from their boats before clubbing or shooting a seal and dragging it back."

One fisherman described doing this last year from 4 a.m. until nightfall for a week, during which he made $320. As dismal as that sounds, failure is defined not as coming back empty-handed, but as falling into the water and dying of hypothermia — not a bad way to go, actually, but still less attractive than sitting around a warm fire and watching the Bruins play the Leafs.

Apparently, fishing the North Atlantic, which just has to be one of the worst jobs on the planet even in the best of times, now leaves its practitioners so impecunious that they have to resort to seal bopping every spring. Think about *that* the next time you're feeling sorry for yourself because some judge yelled at you.

And what does all this have to do with the Doctrine of Unintended Consequences? Well, it turns out that the decline in the seal concussing business is based not just on the fact that seal pelts are now primarily in demand as Montgomery Street paintball targets, but also on the fact that the previously lucrative market for seal penises has ... well ... shriveled up: "Sales are 'way down' from a

---

7 - Yes, it does. It says, "seal penis industry," just as plain as day.

few years ago, says Sang-Jo Chung, who runs an herbal remedies shop in Toronto's Korean district. Mr. Chung points to a leathery 10-inch seal penis on display in a glass case, which he says has been sitting unsold for more than four months."

Can you imagine? How can a 10-inch seal penis go unsold for four months?

Well, according to Mr. Chung, it's the Doctrine of Unintended Consequences.

You see, seal penises are sold as an aphrodisiac. I find this hard to imagine. My experience has been that mere contemplation of a "leathery 10-inch seal penis" depresses ALL my appetites. I forget about food, drink, sex, sleep, chocolate — everything. All I want to do is get that picture out of my mind somehow.

But I am apparently not typical.[8] It seems that seal penises were a very hot aphrodisiacal item in some Asian cultures (at $100 a pop) until Viagra came along. Money was being made hand over fist[9] in Toronto, Newfoundland and points east.

But, in developing a drug to solve the dilemma of male erectile dysfunction,[10] the pharmaceutical industry came up with an easier solution than pinniped genitalia. And in so doing, it unintentionally depressed its sister industry: the seasonal murder of Newfoundland seals and fishermen.

The Journal expressed the problem succinctly but disturbingly. With Viagra on the market, "People can just see a doctor and pop a pill, whereas seal penises are often boiled, which can be smelly, and added to soup or wine."

Soup or wine? They're adding "smelly" seal penises to soup or wine? Jeez, forget the seal clubbers, the industry that's gonna be depressed by this story is Asian restaurants. They're gonna have to post signs: "This establishment does not put seal penises in the soup."

Can you imagine spending a hundred bucks to have boiled seal

---

8 - Who knew?

9 - I know this sounds like some kind of sleazy double entendre, but it's really just another example of my lack of rewrite time. Don't blame me, blame the Commission on Judicial Performance.

10 - The dilemma being which is worse, a man without an erection or a man with one?

penis tossed into your soup? In my whole life (which includes the years 1962-1968, when I thought of almost nothing *but* sex) I never wanted it bad enough to swallow seal penis soup.

So I'm betting the folks at Pfizer pharmaceuticals had no idea when they tried to help out the 30 million men who have this problem[11] that they would be putting a bunch of poor fishermen and Asian herbalists out of business. I'm pretty sure they had no intention of sticking poor Mr. Chung with a smelly, unmovable inventory. Nor did they desire to leave the Newfie fishermen without reason or recompense for all that uninsured ice-floe-cavorting.

But the Doctrine of Unintended Consequences is implacable and unforgiving. I can already see the class actions on the horizon. Attractive plaintiffs (downtrodden working men and women, honest merchants), deep-pocketed defendants, sex (penises), violence (seals), drugs, race. ... Heck, I'd try this one myself. I figure Pfizer stock is gonna go down faster than the Edmund Fitzgerald.

And I am appropriately chastened. I figure if a lot of smart folks like the people at Pfizer can get waylaid trying to do good, I'm pretty vulnerable myself. I figure the Doctrine of Unintended Consequences can get you no matter how good your intentions. So don't look for a lot of published opinions out of me for a while. ❖

— May 2001

---

[11] - That's Pfizer's figure. I've never counted. And based on my conversations with other guys, I've never met one.

Moby Book

California's great blue sesquicentennial whale

I've been remiss.

Turns out it's been four years since I checked the Government Code for the status of our statutory state stuff: you know, the things the Legislature has designated important enough to merit legal recognition as official, like the "State Reptile" (desert tortoise, 1972) and the "State Fish" (California golden trout, 1947).

I don't know how I let this happen. Government Code Sections 420 et seq. are among the most important of our laws. Years ago I promised myself I would keep up on them for the sake of my readership.

I have failed. *Mea culpa, mea culpa, mea maxima culpa.* While I've been asleep at the switch, we've had two important additions to the California Roster of Things the Legislature Thought Were More Important Than Getting Power Deregulation Right, and I have failed to inform you of them.

I'm devastated by my dereliction in this regard. I know you've come to rely upon me to keep you apprised when the Legislature decides we need a "State Prehistoric Artifact" (the chipped stone bear, 1991) or a "State Folk Dance" (the square dance, 1988). I know that without me you might get the "State Rock" (serpentine, 1965) confused with the "State Mineral" (gold, 1965) or even the "State Gemstone" (benitoite, 1985).[1]

Indeed, you might even transgress one of the statutory arcana the Legislature has enacted to protect our "State Fossil" (*Smilodon californicus*,[2] 1973) or our "State Insect" (dogface butterfly, 1972), or one of the two dozen other Official Things the Legislature has foisted upon us over the years.

You might, for example, violate the prohibition on commercial collection of *Hypsypops rubicundus*. Ol' Hypsypops[3] is the official "State Marine Fish" of California. Has been since 1995. And it's been illegal ever since then to catch the little buggers commercially. Honest.

Or you might take benitoite out of season. That's right, "out of season." In California, once you become an Official Thing, you get protection — even if you're a gemstone. "Mining for benitoite is limited to six to eight weeks in March and April due to lack of water." Has been since 1985.

I find this to be a remarkable rule. I can understand limiting when animals can be hunted or fish can be taken or poppies can be picked, but I have no idea how "lack of water" could limit your mining for benitoite. Seems to me we could just "let them drink Coke."

But apparently there's more to it than that. I know mining for benitoite is limited because it says so in my copy of the California Blue Book (1850-2000) Sesquicentennial Edition, which I just got in the mail.[4] Unfortunately, the book does not say what water is limited, why it isn't limited for six weeks in March and April, or why it can't just be brought in on a Sparkletts truck. Which is remarkable because the California Blue Book (1850-2000) Sesquicentennial Edition (*Bookus humongous*, 2001) leaves out almost nothing else.

---

1 - Honest, these are all in Government Code Sections 420 *et sequitur usque ad nauseam.*

2 - *Smilodon californicus* is the scientific designation of the sabre-tooth cat. *Smilodon*. Picture the dental work of a sabre-tooth cat and tell me scientists have no sense of humor.

3 - Also known as the "garibaldi," "a golden orange fish approximately 14 inches in length." And no, I don't know why a fish native to California waters would have an Italian name.

4 - This huge tome is compiled by the California secretary of state's office and mailed, I guess, to all elected officials. That means it's a gift to me from you. Thank you.

I cannot begin to tell you how pleased I was to get my California Blue Book (1850-2000) Sesquicentennial Edition. I had not ordered it, not requested it, not paid for it, never heard of it. It just showed up on my doorstep like some colossal encyclopedic foundling.

But I was thrilled to get it. After all, until now I had no ready reference for the correct spelling of "sesquicentennial." Nor did I have a handy way of determining who was the state assemblyman from Kings County in 1913.[5] I did not know that the Burns-Porter Water Act of 1959 was not named after George Burns and Cole Porter.[6] And I was completely bereft of color photos of the honchos of all our state agencies. Did you know that Patrick Lenz, executive vice chancellor of the board of governors of the California community colleges, sports a really cool Vandyke? Or that Maj. Gen. Paul Monroe Jr., adjutant general of the California Military Department, has a mustache?

I didn't. Hell, I didn't even know we had a military department. I guess if I'd thought about it, I would have realized that the 16,500 members of the Army National Guard, the 4,900 members of the Air National Guard and the 396 members of the apparently more selective State Military Reserve[7] had to have a bureaucracy of some sort to answer to. But I didn't think about it.

Which is why I was so happy to get my 267-pound copy of Moby Book, the Great Blue Sesquicentennial Whale. I now have about six trillion words, punctuated with highly glossy photos, to think about. I haven't turned out an opinion in two weeks. I've been way too busy poring over the list of all the sessions of the state Legislature since 1849. Did you know that in 1935 they met from Jan. 7-26 and then again from March 4-June 16? Says so right here on page 363.

And page 363 isn't even the halfway point. It's a big book. The forklift driver who delivered it was kind enough to explain that while some people had called it a coffee table book, he was pretty sure mine wouldn't hold it. He was right. I'm concerned the *floor* may not hold it. Remember Rulon Gardner, the American weightlifter who upset the Russian in the superheavyweight classification in the

---

5 - J. W. Guiberson. Page 584.

6 - State Sen. Hugh Burns and state Assemblyman Carley Porter. Page 50.

7 - Page 493.

Olympics? Smaller than the book.

But it has to be big to hold all this good stuff. It has a full-page picture of the Jesse M. Unruh Building juxtaposed with a full-page picture of the Library and Courts Building. It's like an architectural centerfold: You get to pages 384-385, and there they are, sprawled provocatively across the pages in all their marble, Ionic columnar, Greek-revival splendor.[8]

And if you turn just a few more of *El Gigantesco Libro Azul Sesquicentenario*'s 772 pages, you can see pictures of all the appellate court justices.[9] In color.

Except Paul Turner, about whom we're cryptically told there was "No Photo Available." This, of course, is ridiculous. Paul Turner is the ambassador plenipotentiary of the Second District Court of Appeal. He goes to every swearing-in, retirement party, bris and supermarket ribbon-cutting in California. I hardly know the man and I'll bet I've got a half-dozen pictures of him from court events I've attended. Pictures of Paul Turner are about as hard to come by as Chicken McNuggets. No, the truth is that a cruel value judgment was made here, and I want to be on record as saying I, for one, do not think Paul Turner was too ugly for the California Blue Book.

I also want to be on record as saying Madera County has the coolest county seal in the entire state.[10] It's actually formed in the shape of the county — and unless you have a map of Madera[11], you can't begin to appreciate what an artistic and geometric challenge it was to get anything into that shape.

The biggest disappointment in the book is that California's "Official State Song" is still "I Love You California," a decision made in 1951 by a bunch of legislators apparently unfamiliar with the concept of music.

---

8 - These two buildings are harder to tell apart than fruitflies, so I'll give you a tip gleaned from an entire morning of studying their virtually identical photos: The Courts Building has horses in the frieze, the Unruh Building has pigs and cows. So if you're looking for bas-relief of pigs and cows, don't go to the Supreme Court. But then, "Don't go to the Supreme Court" is probably advice you didn't need.

9 - Now there's a thrill.

10 - Page 599.

11 - Which I now do. Page 195.

Here is a sample — and a pretty representative sample, at that — of the "Official State Song of California": "I love you, Catalina, you are very dear to me; I love you Tamalpais, and I love Yosemite. I love you, Land of Sunshine, half your beauties are untold; I love you in my childhood, and I'll love you when I'm old."

I'm sorry, but it's beyond me how that could be the "Official State Song" when "Smuggler's Blues," and "Up Against the Wall, Redneck Mothers" are available.[12]

Which brings me back to the Official State Stuff I forgot to tell you about. Turns out that while I was napping, the California Legislature adopted "San Joaquin Soil" as the "State Soil."[13] That's right; we now have official dirt.

See, this is why I'm not cut out for legislative work. I just wouldn't know where to begin in choosing official dirt. There must be so many possibilities.

According to Big Blue, "San Joaquin soils are well- and moderately well-drained, have medium to very high runoff, and have very slow permeability." That certainly sounds impressive, but I'm sure similar encomia could be collected for Placer County tailings or Imperial Valley loam or the infield at Dodger Stadium. Thank God we were blessed in 1997 by a Legislature that knew what it was doing.[14]

Especially since it went so far as to choose the official "State Fife and Drum Band" that year. It chose the California Consolidated Drum Band. This is, of course, one of the most awesome responsibilities settled upon the legislative branch. We're fortunate the choice was so clear in this case. I mean, you just can't get better fifing and drumming than the CCDB. I think we can all agree this was a no-brainer.

---

12 - Nor can I figure out which "half" of our state's beauties are untold now that I've been given a book only slightly smaller than Mount Rushmore extolling everything but the curb in front of the Redwood City Burger King.

13 - Government Code Section 425.9.

14 - Just when did they pass the deregulation thing?

Speaking of which, let me share with you the letter that came with my copy of *El Tremendo Mas Grande Que el Diccionario*. It is on the official letterhead of the secretary of the Senate[15], whom I now know to be Gregory Schmidt, a very pleasant-looking man who dresses nicely and has grandchildren named Kai and Jaden.[16]

It says:

> The Office of the Secretary of the Senate is pleased to present the California Blue Book for 2000. As you may be aware, this publication is required by law but has not been produced since 1975.

Come again?

"Required by law but has not been produced since 1975." I don't know, maybe I spent too long in the district attorney's office, but that seems to me to come perilously close to an admission of guilt. It's hard to believe that nowhere in Sacramento (population: 1,159,800[17]) was there a single lawyer to advise Mr. Schmidt not to write those sentences.

What do you suppose are the elements of the crime of "Ignoring a Legislative Mandate for 25 Years"? Why would the Legislature order this book be published every four years[18] and then ignore its nonpublication for 25 years? And why would the secretary of the senate be selected as the guy to throw himself on the hand grenade and send out a letter to every elected official in the state copping out to the failure to publish?

As usual, I have many questions and damned few answers. But I fully expect the Legislature to take appropriate steps to sort out these questions. I expect a full investigation, a round of hard-hitting committee hearings, followed by decisive action. I figure they'll declare this the official "State Conundrum."

---

15 - I misread this at first and thought it said secretary of state. I thought there had been a coup d'etat and Bill Jones had been defenestrated. I was greatly relieved, upon closer reading of the letterhead, to see that I'd been mistaken.

16 - Page 218.

17 - Page 639.

18 - Government Code Section 14885. Honest. Page 2.

Look for it in the next blue book. Right next to the official "State Taxidermically Preserved Ex-Judge."[19] ❖

— August 2001

---

19 - Copies of the California Blue Book (1850-2000) Sesquicentennial Edition, can be obtained from the Legislative Bill Room, B32 State Capitol, Sacramento, CA 95814. Just in time for the holidays.

My Defining Moment

Summer is here: Don't forget to prune your hysteropotmoi

I had to look up the phrase "hypothetical yearly tenancy" the other day. Now right away you know this Court of Appeal gig is not all it's cracked up to be.

Jobs that require you to sweep out the stables or say no to rock stars or get bitten by spiders regularly might still be good jobs. A job that requires you to look up "hypothetical yearly tenancy" cannot possibly pay enough.

I tried to avoid looking the phrase up. First, I tried to figure it out using nothing more authoritative than my own mind.[1]

I mean, these were three words with which I was reasonably conversant. They weren't especially difficult words, and I had used each of them regularly throughout my career. But try as I might, I couldn't begin to figure out what their juxtaposition could signify.

It was as if I'd been going through a cookbook and came across the phrase "oyster crockpot sommelier." I knew what the words meant; I just couldn't put them together and get anything but dissonance.

But a federal circuit court had made sense of them in a case I need-

---

1- And you don't get a whole lot less authoritative than that.

ed to understand, so I had to somehow mold them into a form that was recognizable in my cosmos. I gave it my best shot.

"Hypothetical yearly tenancy." All right, this is where you theorize about what life would be like if you lived for a year in a rented condo in Boise.

No? OK, it's when you call an expert to assume the existence of a one-year lease and then ask him inane questions about it.

No? Then it's pretending the year only has five months because you're living on Mercury. (I thought this one had promise, since federal circuit judges are almost certainly extraterrestrial, and might therefore have occasion for hypothetical extraterrestrial year calculations, but it just didn't fit in the context of the case.)

I finally had to make two unhappy admissions. First, I had not the slightest idea what the phrase meant. And second, I had no law clerk who'd transgressed in any way that would justify saddling him with it. I had to look it up myself.

So I pulled my Black's off the shelf, shoveled 6 cubic yards of dust off it, and paged halfway into the longest plotless work ever written by someone not named Michener. Sure enough, there it was: hypothetical yearly tenancy, "The basis, in England, of rating lands and hereditaments to the poor-rate, and to other rates and taxes that are expressed to be leviable or assessable in like manner as the poor-rate."

Say what?

Now I was confused. I closed the book and looked at the cover to make sure I had not picked up Black's English-to-Some-Other-Language-You've-Never-Previously-Encountered Dictionary.

"Rating lands and hereditaments to the poor-rate?" "Expressed to be leviable or assessable in like manner?" Who wrote this, Chewbacca the Wookie? You could hold a Sanskrit computer program up to a mirror and read every third word and it would make more sense than this.

These were most definitely words I was not reasonably conversant with.[2] Nor was my spell-check program. My page as I type this is covered with little red worms under questionable words. It looks like a manuscript viewed through the eyes of Keith Richards after a

---

2 - Although I have now renamed my fantasy baseball team the "Laguna Beach Hereditaments."

Stones concert.

Go ahead. Read it again. Is this, or is it not, the legal equivalent of "Fold Flap A across Tab 3 and staple both to opposite ends of the appropriate snipe flanges?" This has to be the same guy who ghost-wrote *Daubert v. Merrill-Dow Pharmaceuticals*. I thought Casey Stengel was dead.

I read it a half-dozen times and then just started laughing. This has to be somebody's idea of a joke. Somebody at the Black's Law Dictionary Co. won a bet on this one. I figure when this edition was published, one of the researchers turned to the guy in the next cubicle and said, "Pay me, Antonin; I told you the editors never read what we write."

And Antonin, cursing softly as he handed over the twenty, grumbled, "Fluke. Just a gawddammed fluke. You couldn't do it again if your life depended on it."

"Do it again?" Abelard the Wordsmith roared. "I could do it 50 times. I've already convinced 'em that 'hwata' or 'hwatung' means, 'In old English law. Augury; divination.' I've already gotten 'em to publish 'Hypobolum' with the explanation that it was the name of the 'bequest or legacy given by the husband to his wife, at his death, above her dowry.'"

"'Hwatung' and 'hypobolum,' Antonin. You know how I got 'hwatung'? I banged all my fingers down on the keyboard at once and held them there for a count of three. My fingers made that word up. If they believed those, they'll believe anything. In fact, I don't think we have editors anymore. I think whatever we write just goes to the janitor and he gets paid an extra 50 dollars a month for alphabetizing 'em."

And Antonin, loyal company man that he was[3], said, "I got another twenty says you can't do it again."

So Abelard, envisioning another night of Guinness instead of Budweiser, threw back his head in laughter and said, "Make it $40 and I'll do it on the same page! I'll make up a word nobody could ever, not for a New York minute, think was a real word. And then I'll make up a definition — the dumbest, most unbelievable, most palpably

3 - But admittedly shaken to realize that "hwatung" was in Black's as an old English word rather than a province in China.

laughable definition since the Scots invented curling[4] — and I'll put the dumb made-up word and the even dumber made-up definition on the same page as the 'hypothetical yearly tenancy' and our editors will swallow it hook, line, sinker, rod, reel, bass boat and Chevy Suburban. You just watch."

And that, boys and girls, has to be how the word, hysteropotmoi made it into the fifth edition of Black's Law Dictionary.

Yep, there it is. Just one word away from "hypothetical yearly tenancy." The word that cost poor, loyal, straight-arrow Antonin 40 bucks because the idiot editors left it in. Right there on page 743 of Black's Law Dictionary: hysteropotmoi.

Is that a real word? Oh, absolutely. I'm sure of it. Let's see, "hystero" from the Greek hysterikos, indicating a delusion. And "pot" from the Latin potare, meaning to drink. And "moi" from the French word for me.

So "hysteropotmoi" would be a delusionary state in which the sufferer believes others are trying to drink her. Of course. Actually, that was a lot easier than the "hypothetical yearly tenancy" thing.

But that's not the definition Black's has. Oh no. You wanna know what Black's says? You wanna know what Abelard actually got the editors of Black's Law Dictionary to sign off on? All right, here it is:

"Those who, having been thought dead, had, after a long absence in foreign countries, returned safely home; or those who, having been thought dead in battle, had afterwards unexpectedly escaped from their enemies and returned home. These, among the Romans, were not permitted to enter their own houses at the door, but were received at a passage opened in the roof."

"A passage opened in the roof"? "A passage opened in the roof"?! Oh, sure. I can picture this without a whole lot of trouble. Guy comes home from five years of battling Ostrogoths and his wife greets him at the door and says, "Gee, Hon,[5] you've been gone so long, we

---

4 - A game in which rocks with handles on them (yes, handles) are pushed across an ice surface toward a shuffleboard goal while players try to adjust their course (the rocks' course, not the players') by melting the ice by sweeping it with brooms so fast that friction melts it. Honest. This one's not in Black's Law Dictionary, it's on Canadian television, so I'm pretty sure it exists.

5 - Or, "Hun," as the case may be.

thought you were dead. I'm afraid I'm remarried to Fergie the Langobard. You'll have to enter through a hole in the roof until we get this all sorted out." Oh, hell yeah, probably happened all the time.

How could they print that? How could anybody think that was a real word? What was going on in their brapscraggins?[6]

As you can tell, I'm pretty upset about this whole thing. I mean, I expect basketball players and anchorwomen and sword-swallowers to have more fun than I do, but philologists?!

There's a lot more I could say about this, but I don't have the time. I gotta go work on my car. Johnson rod broke yesterday and sheared a Knudsen nut right off. I'll be working on it all day. You wouldn't know anybody who has a set of metric Trahorn wrenches would you? ❖

— May 2001

---

6 - A word that would have been in the next edition of Black's if Abelard hadn't tired of this game and taken a job in advertising.

Meal Locks, Maridomes and Brazoria

Why I could never be a federal judge

My friend Dave Carter is now a federal district judge. This is very disconcerting. I'm pretty sure it's only been 10 or 12 years since I graduated from college, so I'm way too young to have contemporaries on the federal bench. Carter must be way older than I thought.

And if he isn't now, he soon will be. The federal bench can age a man.[1]

I went by his place the other night and his den looked like one of those trailer parks you see on TV after the tornado goes through. Files and papers were scattered about as randomly as Bill Clinton picks partners.

Dave picked up a document. "You know what this is?" he asked. "It's the Warsaw Treaty. I've got a case that involves the Warsaw Treaty." Needless to say, I was impressed, although I think the Warsaw Treaty ended the War of 1812, and I'm disappointed that Dave's lawyers couldn't find more recent authority.

I've never had a case that involved a treaty. I had one once that involved a street gang ceasefire violation, but I suspect somehow that the protocol is more formal in Dave's case. His case probably doesn't involve any witnesses who have to explain the significance of their tattoos.

Federal judges get stuck figuring out this kind of … stuff … all the time. Here is a one-sentence summary from the Daily Journal Daily Appellate Report which pretty much explains why I could not be a

---

1 - Women not so much. Hi Alice. Hi Nora.

federal judge[2]. It says, "*Warn v. M/Y Maridome*. Foreign maritime law, rather than the Jones Act, applies where accident involving yacht flying British flag occurs in Grecian waters."

This is a case involving a British-registered yacht, owned by a Mexican citizen, piloted by an American, which runs aground in a Greek harbor, killing British crewmen and German-Greek (dual citizenship) guests. This isn't a case; it's a law school exam question drafted by Stephen King and Charles Manson.

Judge Rudi Brewster got this case. I don't know Rudi Brewster, but I know he's a better man than I. I know this because he did not jump out a window the second this case came across his desk.

What's even more impressive, Judge Brewster held — correctly, according to the Ninth Circuit — that Greek maritime law applied. Do you have any idea what kind of courage it takes to rule that Greek maritime law is to be applied in a case? A case YOU are going to try!

That's why I couldn't be a federal district judge. Not only do I have no more chance of understanding Greek maritime law than your average dolphin, I don't have the ... *huevos* ... to rule that it applies. If I'd been in Rudi Brewster's chair, and this case came my way, I would have ruled that the Jones Act covered the dispute. In a heartbeat. Wouldn't have needed to crack a book.

The reasoning process would have gone like this: Let's see, Jones Act, written in English, by Americans, for Americans, in 1915. Grecian maritime law, written in Greek, probably by Homer, and examined by a half-dozen Americans this century, all of whom died mysteriously, mumbling something about Hector's curse. Jones Act. Clearly, Jones Act.[3]

I'm not sure I'd want much to do with treaty interpretation, even if it didn't involve a whole lot of furriers. Today's Daily Journal includes the case of *Minnesota v. Mille Lacs Band of Chippewa*

---

2 - All right, ONE of the reasons I could not be a federal judge.

3 - Now you cynics — at least those of you who take the time to read the case — might point out that reference to Greek maritime law allowed Judge Brewster to dismiss on grounds of *forum non conveniens*. But that's just cynicism. I'm sure he didn't realize dismissal would be warranted until AFTER he studied Greek maritime law. Besides, if he was smart enough to figure that out ahead of time, he's way ahead of me and the dolphins, and oughta be applauded for his foresight.

Indians. This one's as American as it could be[4], and I still wouldn't go near it without a gallon of antivenom.

Here's how the DJDAR describes this case, "Under the 1837 Treaty, Chippewa Indians retain usufructuary rights to ceded land in present-day Minnesota despite state's 1858 admission to the union." Well of course they do. Who could have doubted it?

Does this sound like a case you'd want to get involved with? Doesn't this sound like every case you were ever handed by a name partner? Doesn't it sound like something that would make you want to reconsider your decision not to go into the aluminum siding business with your Uncle Floyd?

This case is a handful of snakes. Seems the Thousand Lake Indians[5] signed a treaty in 1837 in which they gave up a couple of dozen counties in Minnesota and Wisconsin in exchange for hunting, fishing and gathering rights on the land. Well now, that's a nice even trade. The record does not disclose how many heads were involved. And, as if this weren't illusory enough, those hunting, fishing and gathering rights were to last "during the pleasure of the President of the United States."

Under the present administration, the term "during the pleasure of the President of the United States" would seem to be a grant in perpetuity. But Martin Van Buren was president when this treaty was signed, and pleasure was not as big a part of his presidency as it seems to be today.

So in 1850, President Zachary Taylor declared presidential pleasure over — don't we wish — and ordered the Chippewas off the land. What's more, he "revoked their usufructuary rights."[6]

This, of course, outraged the Thousand Lakes Band because they were using fructuaries on a daily basis. But the rest of the Chippewas were too busy hunting and gathering in the 400 square yards of

---

4 - Except, of course, for the Francification of the Thousand Lakes Band of Indians' name. Milles Lacs, indeed. Sounds like something you put on the refrigerator when you go on a diet.

5 - Apparently they're not yet Native Americans in some quarters.

6 - This is the Supreme Court's term, not President Taylor's. Taylor's nickname was "Old Rough and Ready." In the whole history of the planet, no one called "Old Rough and Ready" has ever spoken the word "usufructuary."

downtown Minneapolis which the treaty left to them to join in a lawsuit, so nothing was done about it.

Until 1990. That's when the Indians went to whoever the Eighth Circuit's equivalent of Rudi Brewster is and saddled him/her with the Sisyphean challenge of determining what President Taylor had in mind in his 1850 executive order declaring the end of his pleasure[7] and whether it made any difference that Minnesota was admitted to the union eight years later without any mention of the treaty or the executive order.

Can you imagine? You're sitting in your chambers, minding your own business, trying to figure out if your grip is too strong to hit a consistent Calcavecchia fade, when your clerk brings word that you've been assigned the task of figuring out what was going on in Zachary Taylor's head[8] in 1850, and what was going on in the heads of a bunch of nameless bureaucrats in 1858. *Bon chance, mon ami!*[9]

Apparently the federal types can really get their heads around this stuff. Justice O'Connor delivered the opinion of the Supreme Court in the case, which, as I read it, gives the Indians the right to hunt deer and gather acorns anywhere between the corner of Busby and Ninth in St. Paul, Minn., and St. Cecilia Catholic Church in Madison, Wis.

Chief Justice Rehnquist dissented on the basis that President Taylor could not have been acting in an official capacity when he issued the executive order, since research disclosed that none of his garments had three stripes on the sleeves. And Justice Thomas dissented because of his longstanding policy that any case involving Minnesota should mention Kirby Puckett.

At least that's what I get out of 99 Daily Journal DAR 2735, but then again, I've already expressed my difficulty in mustering up the intellectual horsepower these cases require, so you might want to take a look at it for yourself.

This is not to say, however, that I couldn't handle ANY of the cases my federal brethren and cistern[10] deal with. Judge Samuel Kent of

---

7 - Insert your own snide, tasteless Bill Clinton joke here. I'm tired of them.

8 - A task which may very well REQUIRE that you assume facts not in evidence.

9 - The Meal Locks Indians thing kinda inspired me.

10 - I'm no longer explaining that "cistern" is the plural form of "sister" just as "brethren" is the plural form of brother. I figure if you don't know this by now you're not a regular reader and therefore don't deserve my attention.

Galveston, Texas, recently dealt with a matter I could have gotten right. But I could never have disposed of it as eloquently as he did.

Kent is the only federal district judge in the Southern District of Texas. The southern district, most notably Brazoria County, is a plaintiff's paradise. So it probably did not come as too big a surprise to Kent that when the Republic of Bolivia decided to climb aboard the gravy train that is litigation against the tobacco companies, they filed their lawsuit there. Contemplating a defendant who does business everywhere in America, and finding no federal districts made up entirely of hospital cancer wards, Bolivia chose Brazoria County, Texas, as the most favorable venue available.

I don't know if Judge Kent had to take the tobacco out of his cheek to get his tongue into it, but his ruling is the stuff of which Texas legend is made. He said, according to The Wall Street Journal,[11] "[T]he court can hardly imagine why the Republic of Bolivia elected to file suit in the veritable hinterlands of Brazoria County, Texas. The court seriously doubts whether Brazoria County has ever seen a live Bolivian ... even on the Discovery Channel. Though only here by removal, this humble court by the sea is certainly flattered by what must be the worldwide renown of rural Texas courts for dispensing justice with unparalled fairness and alacrity, apparently in common discussion even on the mountain peaks of Bolivia! Still, the court would be remiss in accepting an obligation for which it truly does not have the necessary resources. ...

"And while Galveston is indeed an international seaport, the capacity of this court to address the complex and sophisticated issues of international law and foreign relations presented by this case is dwarfed by that of its esteemed colleagues in the District of Columbia who deftly address such awesome tasks as a matter of course. ... Such a bench, well populated with genuinely renowned intellects, can certainly better bear and share the burden of multidistrict litigation than this single judge division, where the judge moves his lips when he reads. ...

"Plaintiff has an embassy in Washington, D.C., and thus a physical presence and governmental representation there, whereas there

---

[11] - No, of course not. The Wall Street Journal has no pictures and lousy hockey coverage. I'd rather read the Djakarta Pennysaver. But Jennifer Keller reads it, and she shares.

isn't even a Bolivian restaurant anywhere near here. Although the jurisdiction of the court boasts no similar foreign offices, a somewhat dated globe is within its possession. While the court does not therefrom profess to understand all of the political subtleties of the geographical transmogrifications ongoing in Eastern Europe, the court is virtually certain that Bolivia is not within the four counties over which this court presides, even though the words Bolivia and Brazoria are a lot alike and caused some real, initial confusion until the court conferred with its law clerks. Thus, it is readily apparent, even from an outdated globe such as that possessed by this court, that Bolivia, a hemisphere away, ain't in south-central Texas, and that, at the very least, the District of Columbia is a more appropriate venue (though Bolivia isn't located there either). Furthermore, as this judicial district bears no significant relationship to any of the matters at issue, and the judge of this court simply loves cigars, the plaintiff can be expected to suffer neither harm nor prejudice by a transfer to Washington, D.C., a bench better able to rise to the smoky challenges presented by this case despite the alleged and historic presence there of countless 'smoke-filled' rooms."

If I could write like that, I might want to be a federal judge. As it is, I'll just settle for plagiary. Which is probably a federal crime. I'll get sent to Dave Carter. He'll try to fit me in between his bottomry cases.[12] Poor Dave. ❖

---

12 - Look it up. Dave will.

Silence Is ... Well, Golden

A recent settlement has our columnist listening to the music of the spheres

I'm not sure I'm up to this one. I've found a settlement so completely beyond my ability to comprehend that I'm afraid it may also be beyond my ability to describe. I feel a little like a baby ferret who's come across an ostrich egg: my instincts tell me it's food, but I have no idea how to go about eating it.

This is what I get for reading the Arts and Entertainment section of the paper. I should know better. This is not my turf. I have about as much chance of understanding people who write about the fine arts as I have of running wires from a wok to my television set and contacting Venusians. I should have realized that even lawsuits discussed there would be alien to me.

But I was sucked in by the word "settlement" — which is a word I understand — and the words "Pop/Rock" which is the only music not involving a dobro guitar which I feel capable of discussing. Besides, the article is only 159 words long. What's not to understand?

As it turned out, about 157 words.

According to the article — and I'm pretty sure of this because I have read it 27 times forward, three times backward, and once skipping every other word, desperately trying to make sense of it[1] — a British rock musician has agreed to pay "six figures" to the estate of a dead composer in settlement of the composer's estate's lawsuit against him. The offense which called for this rather hefty expiation was including "a minute devoid of sound on 'Classical Graffiti,' the latest album by his rock group, the Planets."

That's right. According to the Los Angeles Times, "[Michael] Batt agreed Monday to pay an undisclosed sum to the John Cage Trust, after publishers of the late American composer sued him for compensation, claiming he had plagiarized Cage's 1952 composition, '4'33",' which was totally silent."

Say what?

So help me, every time I read this, my jaw drops all the way to my desk and I have to backspace to erase the word, "jnmhjk," which turns out to be what my chin types when it bounces twice on my keyboard.

There is nothing I understand about that sentence. It seems to say that a reputable composer copyrighted four minutes and thirty-three seconds of silence and someone else infringed that copyright by being silent for one minute. If that makes sense to you, I welcome you to the planet and beg you to take pity on my fellow earthlings, because we are clearly not as advanced as life on your planet.

Me, I woulda bet the mortgage this was an "Ally McBeal" plot line. I mean, I know when my leg is being pulled, and this one gives me a huge pain in the ... hip.

I know there are composers who are too cerebral for me. Ives, Stravinsky, even some of Copland, all appeal a little too much to my gray matter and not enough to my ears. I readily admit their stuff goes over my head.

But silence doesn't go over my head. It goes right through it. Without a scintilla of comprehension. I just don't get it.

In the first place, how do you "compose" four minutes and thirty-three seconds of silence?[2] What system of musical notation do you use to record your "work?" How do you determine where it begins

---

1 - The every other word thing worked best, but I'm not real confident about it because it's never worked before.

2 - And having composed it, how do we encourage rappers (note that I don't use the oxymoron "rap musicians") to sample it?

and where it ends?

If the audience doesn't figure out that it's over and sits quietly for a few seconds (probably stunned), does it become a different piece? Does it become 4'38"? Does their failure to recognize the end of the piece reflect badly on the performer?

And who is that performer? Who was this composition written for? Is it for piano, for orchestra, or for voice?[3] What is it that is not being played[4] during this piece for four minutes and thirty-three seconds? Is "4'33"" different when performed by the Boston Philharmonic than it is when performed by Earl Flatt and Lester Scruggs?

And just how do you get this composition copyrighted? Did someone actually go to the copyright office and say, "Excuse me. I would like to copyright four minutes and thirty-three seconds of silence. I will expect, of course, that any time any musician goes four minutes and thirty-three seconds during a performance without playing, I will receive a royalty check. I'll just leave my application right here; you can mail the copyright to me, thank you very much."

No kidding, I have a real conceptualization problem here. Just what is it the copyright lawyer studies interminably before advising his client whether he infringed on Cage's work — a sheaf of music papers unadorned except for a treble clef, a bass clef, and a coffee stain? Did the lawyer have to verify the length of the piece by comparing the time notation[5] with the number of pages of blank paper he was given and determine whether playing at that speed it would take the requisite 273 seconds to reach the end?

And what did he compare it to? Can't you just imagine a bunch of IP types[6] kicking this around over lunch? "I dunno, Mate, seems to me it sounds an awful lot like Beethoven's Tenth or Rachmaninoff's Fourth. Both of those used silence in a very similar way. Not sure there isn't some plagiarizing going on here."[7]

---

3 - Personally, I hope it's for harp. It would be the first time I was ever able to listen to four and a half minutes of harp music without squirming in my chair.

4 - Or is it "being not played?" The syntax is as impenetrable as the concept.

5 - Let's assume it was written in 3/4 time, since it's easier to waltz to silence than it is to rhumba to it. I'm told.

6 - Gaggle? School? Pride? What is the proper term for groups of IP types?

7 - Imagine their consternation over the fact "Sounds of Silence," by Simon and Garfunkel, was much louder.

But as completely as all of this exceeds my ken, I am even more amazed that the rock musician paid off on this claim. He settled. For six figures — something which would make sense to me only if the first five were zeroes.

Granted, by putting a sock in it for sixty seconds, Batt was arguably plagiarizing almost a fourth of Cage's entire work. Plaintiff was not going to get bogged down here arguing about whether a pair of four or five note motifs from "My Sweet Lord" were indistinguishable from "He's So Fine." The trust could show that an entire minute of Batt's work was absolutely indistinguishable from Cage's. But the whole thing is so damned goofy, it's hard to imagine that identity would be enough to send 12 bus drivers, beekeepers and retired aerospace workers scrambling for their calculators to compute damages.

I mean, think about it. Guy walks into your office. Says, "I'm being sued for plagiarizing another musician's music."

You say, "Lemme hear the pieces."

He says, "Sure. Sit there for a minute imagining me being silent; then sit there for four minutes and thirty-three seconds imagining Chopin being silent. I'm being sued for not making noises that sound just like the noises Chopin didn't make."

Tell the truth. Don't you call security and have that guy escorted from the building?[8]

I do. And then I sit there for 20 minutes wondering if maybe I shouldn't keep a gun in my desk, even though I no longer do family law.

Maybe Michael Batt couldn't find a lawyer who'd listen to him, either. Maybe that's why he settled.

Which had to be great news to the John Cage Trust. Because there's no way you can put this case on.

You could not find 12 adults in America who could listen to four minutes and 33 seconds of silence and then have a lawyer say, "Now compare what you just heard to this minute of nothingness," without bursting into laughter.

And they would laugh every time the "subject compositions" were

---

8 - I chose Chopin for this example because he's been dead longer than Cage. Most of us have about 100 years more experience imagining Chopin silent than imagining Cage silent. If this makes sense to you, you could have handled the lawsuit described above.

"played." Every time. And any plaintiffs lawyer will tell you that your damages go down in direct proportion to the amount of times the jurors fall out of the jury box laughing at your case. I think that's Newton's Third Law of Catastrophic Pyrotechnics (also known as the Crash and Burn Rule). Lawyers who take cases like this not only don't get six-figure settlements, they don't get above the Mendoza Line.[9]

So, at first glance, it seems incomprehensible that Michael Batt, or his insurer, would pay money — real, live, take-it-to-the-store-and-exchange-it-for-peanut-butter-cookies money — and in large amounts, for being silent for a minute. I mean, the theory of the lawsuit was that a minute's silence infringed a copyright of four minutes and 33 seconds of silence. Wouldn't you have wanted to at least fire off an interrogatory asking which minute of the piece you were alleged to have infringed? I think I would have fought this one.

But our boy Batt is no fool. Turns out he's now set a precedent. "Batt has registered copyrights for 4 minutes and 32 seconds of silence and 4 minutes and 34 seconds of silence. ('If there's ever a Cage performance where they come in a second shorter or longer, then it's mine,' he told The New Yorker.)" And when he sues, he's going to be able to point out to them that the last time this issue was raised, it was settled for golfbags full of cash.

I dunno. I still don't like plaintiff's side of this. I think I'd rather have a five-time felon with soft-tissue injuries whose chiropractor once shared a cell with him.

But I gotta admit, these copyright guys seem to roll over a lot quicker than insurance companies. Who knows, maybe silence is golden. ❖

— November 2002

---

9 - Mario Mendoza was a big-field, no-hit shortstop for the Seattle Mariners, whose batting average hovered around .200. His teammates began referrings to this as the "Mendoza Line," and that number — representing four failures in every five tries — has become the benchmark of baseball futility. It is well-known to attorneys who violate Newton's Third Law of Catastrophic Pyrotechnics.

Gods and Godlings

An obscure federal case may explain a lot

Pay attention. This column is actually going to have some redeeming social value. Not a whole lot, but some. Get ready. I want you to read this sentence, from a published opinion of the Ninth Circuit U.S. Court of Appeals, and tell me what about it strikes you as unusual — unusual, that is, even for the Ninth Circuit:

"We believe the controlling issue, however, is whether, as of the time of the publication, the Foundation, the copyright claimant, could trace its title back to the humans who owned the original common law copyright."

You done? All right, what struck you as unusual about that sentence? No, no, besides the six commas.

How about the use of the word "humans." When's the last time you read an opinion in which a court found it necessary to describe the legal position of the "humans?"

Let me just suggest to you that any time you find a court referring to participants in a lawsuit as "humans," you've found yourself an opinion that is not going to be just another roadside attraction. The only reason for referring to the holders of the original copyright as "humans" is to differentiate them from the NON-HUMANS. That's pretty much my definition of a case worth reading.

Which, of course, pretty much assures that it's going to end up with the feds. They get all the really good alien being, spaceship sighting, Elvis is alive and well and working for the CIA in my rec room kind of cases. That's because, under a little-known federal law, they get first choice.

And, of course, the Ninth Circuit gets first choice of all the goofy cases that come out of California, Nevada and Arizona. That's like having a license to mine gold in Fort Knox. I mean, between the half-baked ideas that come out of California and the overcooked ideas that come out of the desert southwest, the Ninth Circuit gets to listen to more craziness than Mick Jagger's therapist. For example, they get cases like *Urantia Foundation v. Maaherra.*

Here are the UNCONTESTED facts of *Urantia Foundation v. Maaherra*, 114 F.3d 955. I took these right out of the court's opinion. Read them and tell me you wouldn't be bitter if the Ninth Circuit kept stealing cases like this from you.

According to the Ninth Circuit, the Urantia Book is a collection of divine revelations, authored by "non-human spiritual beings" including the Divine Counselor, the Chief of the Archangels of Nebadon, and, my personal favorite, the Chief of the Corps of Superuniverse Personalities.

Wouldn't you just love to be the Chief of the Corps of Superuniverse Personalities? I mean, just being a Superuniverse Personality would be really cool. But being the chief of the entire corps, THAT would be a great job.

How many Superuniverse Personalities do you suppose there are? I mean, I figure Dr. Phil is pretty obviously one of them. And John Tesh. Arianna Huffington, maybe. But beyond that, I think they've done an admirable job of cloaking their identities.

Perhaps too good. The revelations of the Superuniverse Personalities *et al.* were divulged through — I am not making this up — the "patient of a Chicago psychiatrist." The Chicago psychiatrist is identified by the Ninth Circuit only as "Dr. Sadler." The name of the patient who actually walked into Dr. Sadler's office with the stone tablets in tow is not divulged, presumably due to patient/psychotherapist privilege.

Isn't it always the way? I mean, if the godhead would just make these pronouncements through the President of the United States or the Speaker of the House of Representatives or Wolf Blitzer, or somebody else we all believe all the time, the whole religion thing would be a lot easier. But She keeps picking people with very little credibility . . . like psychiatrists. This really seems an unnecessary complication of stuff that's already tough enough.

And before I go any further into this, let me hasten to point out I am NOT disparaging anyone's religious beliefs. Do not send me letters about religious intolerance.

Most of my family are Zen Golf-Baptists: They believe dancing is sinful unless you do it in sand and rake up your footprints.

I myself happen to belong to a religion which accepts as fact burning bushes which speak and people who live inside the bellies of large fishes for extended periods of time. My religion is just chock-full of stuff Isaac Newton and Stephen Hawking on their best days couldn't make heads or tails of. Having bought into all of that, I am in no position to indulge in religious bigotry.

Besides, I really know nothing about what these people believe except that it involves a whole crew of archangels I never heard of, and that doesn't bother me a bit. Near as I can determine every religion gets to name its own archangels, just as every major league manager gets to name his own coaches. Seems fair to me. I figure until one of these groups shows up with a notarized document from God, we're free to root for whatever team we want. I lose very little sleep over OTHER people's religious beliefs.

I am, however, seriously frosted about what terrific cases other courts get. I have nothing against the Ninth Circuit — which, as I understand it, disqualifies me for Congress, but that's not a bad deal, either — I just don't understand why they merit this case, while highly qualified deep-thinkers like me plod through the muck of cases involving mere mortals. Why should a court which spends most of its time struggling to get its batting average above the Mendoza line get thrown softballs like this one?

But I digress.

To return to the actual reported decision — a fact which I mention here because I think it's easy to lose sight of the fact that this isn't satire, it's MCLE — Dr. Sadler did what anyone would do when confronted with divine revelation: he formed a committee. He got together "five or six followers, called the Contact Commission."

Personally, I think this was a mistake. I haven't had a lot of truck with commissions in my life, but it seems to me they're always riling folks up. Think about it; you got your Securities and Exchange Commission, your Public Utilities Commission, your police commission, your Warren Commission, and all you ever hear about is how unhappy people are with them. I think any chance you have NOT to form a commission should be taken advantage of, but Dr. Sadler did not ask my advice.

According to the Ninth Circuit, "[A]pparently in response to what they perceived to be prompting from the spiritual beings, and in collaboration with a larger group of followers called the Forum, the Contact Commission began to pose specific questions to the spiritual beings. The answers to these questions, as transmitted to the humans and arranged by them, became the Urantia Papers [also known as "the Book," the subject of this lawsuit]." 114 F.3d 955, 957. Honest.

Things apparently went well at first. Oh, there was the occasional lawsuit brought by covetous non-*Nebadonians* (see, e.g., *Urantia Foundation v. Burton*, 210 U.S.P.Q. 217 (W.D. Mich. 1980)), and the occasional problem with state courts rejecting believers' freedom of religion defenses to their pot-cultivation charges (see, e.g., *People v. Mullins* (1975) 50 Cal.App.3d 61), but nothing more than you'd expect whenever the Divine Counselor is involved.

Until 1990. That's when the folks in charge of the Urantia Book found out someone was distributing it — along with a "study aid," no less — on computer disks. FOR FREE!!

They tracked down defendant Maaherra in Arizona, and sued her for infringing the copyright they had presciently obtained in 1956 and renewed in 1983. Her defense was that their copyright was invalid because, after all, THE BOOK WAS NOT WRITTEN BY HUMANS!

This enabled the Ninth Circuit to break some new ground. They noted that "The copyright laws, of course, do not expressly require 'human' authorship . . .," but nonetheless upheld the Foundation's claim of copyright violation. This required the pronouncement which is perhaps my favorite thing ever said by a federal judge that did not include dinner plans: "We agree with Maaherra, however, that it is not creations of divine beings that the copyright laws were intended to protect, and that in this case some element of human creativity must have occurred in order for the Book to be copyrightable." 114 F.3d 955, 958.

Tell me if I'm reading too much into it, but isn't that a holding that God has no standing on copyright issues? Isn't the Ninth Circuit hanging out a sign on the area of intellectual property that says, "Divine beings need not apply?"

They make it even clearer later in the paragraph: "At the very least, for a worldly entity to be guilty of infringing a copyright, that entity must have copied something created by another worldly entity." Note they don't say "an other-worldly entity," but "another worldly entity." The other-worldly entities are just S.O.L.

I mean, I don't know where these people worship, but I ordinarily make it a practice to try to decide cases without ruling that DEITIES HAVE NO STANDING! Call me timid, but that just seems real risky to me.

I can only assume the Ninth Circuit has decided the U.S. Supreme Court is not a sufficiently worthy adversary and has decided to take on the REAL Supreme Court. Talk about tugging on Superman's cape.

I must confess here that I was too timid to shepardize this case. I wasn't sure whether I'd be more likely to see, "Petition granted," or "Plague of locusts visited upon." I'll leave it to you to determine whether *Urantia Foundation v. Maaherra* is still good law.

But you don't need Shepard's to tell you that anybody who rules God has no standing is not a good person to be standing next to during an electrical storm. And, sure enough, of the three judges who joined in this decision, two (Donald Lay and Mary Schroeder) have been saddled with the chief judgeship of their respective circuits. And the third, Alfred Goodwin, got to decide the Pledge of Allegiance case — not quite a non-stop ticket to hell, but close enough.

So by my lights, none of the godlings who decided this case have been well-treated by the Real Thing since Urantia. Just goes to show you, it may take awhile, but the mills of God do not forget. You deny standing to deities, you get ground exceedingly small. ❖

— October 2002

¡Ay Caramba, Taco Bell!

A $30 million settlement runs from the border of common sense

The big news here in Orange County is that the civil justice system has just filched — or reclaimed, depending on just where you stand on this particular ox-goring — from one of our local corporations the rather impressive sum of $30.2 million. Since we are a county of 3 million people, the economic impact of this judgment is the same as if each of us had just been fined $10.[1]

Taco Bell, which has its logo at the top of one of our tallest buildings, and must therefore be one of our finest corporate citizens, has been ordered to pay $30.2 million to two guys from Grand Rapids, Mich., for stealing their talking dog idea.

Apparently, the talking animal thing isn't yet in the public domain. The two guys from Michigan say they invented the talking Chi-

---

1 - This, of course, is absolute rubbish. It's not the same at all. But since no one understands economics, I figured I could just say anything I wanted and most people wouldn't question it. Tell the truth; if I hadn't stopped you with this footnote, you would have gone blithely past that ridiculous statement, hoping in vain that I was getting ready to say something funny.

huahua and that Taco Bell stole it from them and used it to make people buy tacos.

I'm not sure exactly how that works. I buy a lot of fast food. I like fast food. And I have never in my life decided which kind of fast food to buy based on whether I liked or disliked their commercials.[2]

I don't claim to be the most sophisticated consumer on the block. Maybe the advertising thing is going over my head (a pretty frightening idea when you consider how low it's aimed). But my thought process on fast-food choice goes something like this: I want to eat. What do I want to eat? Where can I get that?

That's it. That's the whole three-step process.

I suspect that's pretty close to the cerebration that precedes most people's decision to pull into a Taco Bell. And advertising has a lot less to do with it than how far we have to drive.

So the idea that I would choose Taco Bell over Del Taco[3] because I liked their spokesdog is so alien to me as to make me wonder if the Svengalis who work in ad agencies employ overt hypnosis or something more subtle — probably involving drugs — to get corporate types to sign these contracts.

George Orwell, who wasted fewer words in his life than I do in a column, once described advertising as "the rattling of a stick inside a swill bucket." This has always seemed to me a rather harsh assessment, but I must admit that talking Chihuahua dogs seem to me only a small step up from the Orwellian model.

Frankly, I can't help wondering if the "99-cent menu" might not be a lot more extensive — or maybe even a "69-cent menu" — if the fast food people weren't spending trash bags full of money on vaguely racist dogs and dancing clowns and the like.[4]

And yet a jury, made up entirely of people whom the state of Michigan trusts to drive cars and vote, decided this was worth $30.2

---

2 - Although Carl's Jr. did frighten me away for a while with the "If it doesn't get all over the place, it doesn't belong in your face" ads, which seemed to me to say, rather clearly, that if you ate their burgers you would become a drooling, sexist moron, unable to eat or otherwise function without assistance.

3 - A decision I am required to make considerably more often than whether appropriate jury instructions were given.

4 - I make an exception here for the Jack-in-the-Box people, whose TV spots of late I view to be not so much advertising as literature.

million. American.

They may be right. Personally, I've continued to eat at Taco Bell despite the stupid talking Chihuahua, so I'm probably not the right guy to assess the value of this advertising campaign. I disliked it so much that if I thought the guys making the food were as stupid as the guys approving the advertising, I would have been afraid to eat at Taco Bell.

But I didn't, so I wasn't. Ultimately, my decision was that while I found the Chihuahua to be the animatronic equivalent of Speedy Gonzales and couldn't begin to fathom why the Mexican-American community wasn't more up in arms about him, if it was cool with it, then I was cool with it.

Besides, I liked the burritos.[5]

But 12 federal jurors in Michigan decided this was intellectual property of considerable value. I find this remarkable for several reasons.

First, it was a talking dog, for crying out loud. It's difficult to watch television for more than two commercial breaks without being confronted with a talking animal of some kind — usually a dog or a cat. These animals have been telling me what dog food to buy or what veterinarian to see or what kitty litter to use for most of my life. I can still remember the "Doctor Ross dog food is doggone good ... woof," ads, and it's been 40 years since the company went out of business. How can anybody still claim a talking dog idea as proprietary?

Second, according to The Orange County Register, "The ad campaign became a favorite of TV viewers nationwide and ran until mid-2000, though it failed to boost Taco Bell's sales. The chain fired its president, Peter Waller, in July 2000." So the jury awarded $30.2 million for an ad campaign that was unsuccessful and cost the company president his job. Just how do you compute damages on something like that?

Third, "Taco Bell's parent, Kentucky-based Yum Brands[6], will

---

5 - This is not a significant endorsement; with the exception of actual small burros, I will pretty much eat any burrito.

6 - These are the people who changed all the Kentucky Fried Chicken outlets to "KFC" because they figured "Kentucky" and "Fried" rang bad subliminal bells in our heads and we were stupid enough that if they just used the letters "KFC," we'd think we were eating arugula and tofu.

take a second-quarter charge of 6 cents a share to account for the verdict." Criminy, how many shares of stock are there in this company, that 6 cents a share will make up $30.2 million? And haven't these people already suffered enough, owning stock in a company represented by Dinky[7] the Chihuahua?

Fourth, Taco Bell executives say they "continue to strongly believe that the Taco Bell Chihuahua character formerly used in our advertising campaign was created by the Chiat/Day advertising agency, not the plaintiffs." What in the world is the factual dispute here?

Taco Bell says Chiat/Day came up with the idea in 1997. The two guys from Michigan say they pitched a talking Chihuahua to Taco Bell in 1996 and worked with them on development of the campaign for 10 months! Ten months! Surely that left a paper trail. How can you work for 10 months with a company on an ad campaign and not have dynamite documentary evidence establishing who invented the thing? How can Taco Bell not know who invented Dinky? And if there is no paper trail, what convinced the Michigan jury? Voices in their fillings?

Of course, the better question is, "How can it take 10 months to come up with, 'The Chihuahua walks into the Taco Bell and says, "Yo quiero Taco Bell."'" But these questions never get asked except in my mind. Maybe they needed a translator.

Anyway, you can imagine my chagrin when I read that Taco Bell's spokeswoman said, "We intend to appeal this decision." Since the corporate headquarters is in Irvine, I was scared to death this case could end up on my desk. You can see how completely unsuited I am to hear it.

But then I read that the feds have it in Michigan. The last time I was this glad something was in Michigan, it was Detroit.

Let the feds have it. They've got lifetime appointments. They have time to figure this stuff out.

But if this verdict is upheld ... and Taco Bell decides that for $30.2 million, it oughta get more mileage out of Dinky ... and he starts showing up on my TV screen again ... then somebody in the Sixth Circuit is gonna have some 'splaining to do. ❖

— July 2003

---

7 · Honest, that's his name.

The Tonga Trust Fund

A case only Bob Gardner could love

Way too much of the best work ever turned out by the California Court of Appeal was written by Justice Robert Gardner. You don't have to take my word for it. You can review the two articles that the Santa Clara University Law Review devoted entirely to his work[1] — articles written by students he didn't know at a school he didn't attend in a county he seldom so much as drove through — and see for yourself. He is also the only man I've ever known who could accurately be described as an *enfant terrible* at the age of 86.

He retired from the Fourth District in 1981. Under duress. The state of California was big on compulsory retirements then, and Bob had reached the magic number. As Bob tells the story, a guy from the AOC showed up and put a gun to his wife's head (her survivor benefits would be forfeited if he did not retire) and he suddenly found himself unemployed.

But Bob landed on his feet. The author of a published book on body surfing, he somehow talked himself into a job as the chief jus-

---

1 - "A Gallery of Gardner," 19 Santa Clara L Rev 925 (1979) and "Gardner: The Second Gallery," 24 Santa Clara L Rev 901 (1984).

tice of the High Court of American Samoa, which, he had noticed, had beaches. There he spent four years soaking up sun and sorting out Samoan property disputes (all I remember about this is that Samoan property descends in the female line and the "records" he encountered were primarily oral and anecdotal) before coming home to do pretty much the same thing on assignment in Newport Beach.

All this comes to mind now because I've just read about a guy named Jesse Bogdonoff who handled the transition from Mainland Suit to South Seas Mucky-Muck with considerably less aplomb than Bob Gardner. As they say in Australia — which is itself a South Seas island — he "made a meal of it."

The story begins in 1994 with Bogdonoff employed by Bank of America to call people up and persuade them to take money out of their T-bills and savings accounts and invest it in investments with a higher rate of return.[2] Since my only connection with the stock market is watching it devour my retirement funds, I can't claim to have any real expertise in such things, but this strikes me as the financial equivalent of the Fuller Brush man: You show up at the door with a pocketful of toilet brushes and mops and try to convince the homeowner that the house is a lot dirtier than he thought. I suspect it was not Bogdonoff's dream job.

Until he ran across the Tonga Trust Fund. Has a nice ring to it, doesn't it? The Tonga Trust Fund.

Tonga is a kingdom[3] of about 112,000 souls.[4] Its chief export, according to the Los Angeles Times, is baby squash.

As far as I know, Tonga is the only place in the world whose chief export is baby squash. I'm not sure about this, but I think you're better off if your chief export is baby diamonds or baby uranium or baby manganese. Baby squash seems a terribly slender reed from which to hang an economy.

---

2 - Of course, this is a euphemism for "investments with a higher rate of risk," but if you describe them like that, you spend a lot of time listening to dial tones.

3 - That's right, a kingdom. Nice looking man whose subjects — judging from his picture on the Web site — must expect him to wear a lot of gold braid.

4 - The Tonga Web site lists a population of 105,600 as of July 1995. Apparently, it hasn't cared enough to recount since then, and with a growth rate of 0.78 percent, there's hardly a pressing need for a new census.

This may explain why kingdom officials devote a large number of bytes on their Web site to trying to lure business. If you move your business there, they will give you a 15-year tax holiday, but they seem to be a little short on paved roads and electricity, so it would probably be best if your business didn't require those things. Bogdonoff says there were pigs loose in the streets the first time he visited.

And they had $20 million in a trust fund in Bank of America. Tonga, that is, not the pigs.

So how did they get $20 million in trust selling baby squash to the Ritz Carlton? Turns out during the '80s, Tonga somehow hit on the idea of selling passports to Hong Kong residents who feared the loss of travel privileges when the former colony reverted to Chinese control. Voila! Twenty million dollars.

Tonga was inexplicably reluctant to transform this money from a trust fund into the ante in a high-stakes poker game. Bogdonoff made a few phone calls ("Excuse me, my name is Jesse Bogdonoff; I work for Bank of America ... in San Francisco ... 11 time zones from you. I'd like to speak to the king, please.") and got nowhere. So he flew to Tonga.

After wending his way through the aforementioned pigs, he was granted an audience with King Taufa'ahau. According to Jesse, they "hit it off." Long story short, Bogdonoff flew home drenched in the $20 million worth of rain he had made and with no greater care in the world than what kind of Champagne would be served at the party in his honor.

Well, all went well for about five years. Bogdonoff says he made $11 million for Tonga.[5] But he was still a Bank of America employee. This is not one of the more obvious roads to spectacular wealth.

And under the terms of his employment contract, he couldn't just fly the coop and take Tonga with him. B of A was apparently willing to let its money managers grab a single brass ring by taking employment with one of its clients, but it wasn't willing to let them jump ship with a whole handful of rings.[6] So its employment contract prohibited Bogdonoff from making Tonga's business his own unless he

5 - Tonga says it was more like $6 million. As we've learned of late, it seems to get harder to keep track of money when there are large sums of it involved. Just ask Arthur Andersen.

6 - Feel free to mix and match metaphors here as you wish. You might also want to throw in a Phil Jackson reference if you're a basketball fan.

went "in house."

No problem. As Jesse explained to the king, he was perfectly suited to an "in-house job" with the kingdom of Tonga. In fact, he had his eye on a position the king had not previously filled. Court jester.

Honest. According to the Times, "In April 1999, according to a royal decree Bogdonoff asked the king to draw up, he became 'King of Jesters and Jester to the King to fulfill his royal duty sharing mirthful wisdom and joy as a special goodwill ambassador to the world.'"

The Times doesn't disclose how much the court jester gig pays. It does mention that Jesse signed another deal — after he had been "employed" as Tonga's court jester for two months — as adviser to the Tonga Trust Fund at a salary of $250,000 per year.

So let's review. Jesse Bogdonoff went from worker bee in the A.P. Giannini hive to court jester/trust fund adviser plenipotentiary of the Kingdom of Tonga in the space of 60 days. This is very cool. I'm sure all you Horatio Alger fans are loving this story.

Unfortunately, it has a sad ending. Litigation.

Yeah. Turns out Jesse put 20 million of Tonga's 26 million eggs into a single basket ... er, company ... called Millennium Asset Management, which planned to make gazillions of dollars "purchasing life insurance policies from senior citizens." You and I can't begin to fathom how this works, but we shouldn't feel bad about that: neither did Millennium.

They fell a little short of the $6 million return on investment Jesse predicted. Twenty-six million short, to be exact. Tonga said in its lawsuit it lost the whole $20 million. Tonga seems upset that they came out of this deal worse than Jesse, who admits he received commissions from Millennium on the $20 million. And, of course, his paycheck from Tonga.

According to Tonga's lawsuit against Jesse, "a second investment was in a company whose stock is now worthless. Another investment involved a high-tech startup that has since filed for bankruptcy." Funny stuff, huh? Tonga's still waiting for the court jester to deliver on the punch line.

Jesse's response to the lawsuit is that it is "frivolous" and an "expression of the incredible incompetence and political intrigue of the children of the royal family. It's typically Tongan." Yeah, leave it to those humorless Pacific Islanders to get all worked up over a paltry

$26 million.

As near as I can make out, Jesse's defense is insanity. He's pictured in the Times wearing a jester's outfit (complete with velvet robe and multi-pointed jester hat). He says he's getting out of the portfolio-crashing business and going into music. "He has his own sound, which he describes as 'a funky, jazzy fusion.'" He says, "I'm gonna keep the identity. There's a certain amount of notoriety," which may help record sales.

Looks to me like the insanity defense is a good one. We had a county controller here in Orange County whose career in portfolio destruction greatly resembles Jesse's. Basically, he sat down at a card table in his penny loafers and argyle sweater to play poker against a bunch of guys wearing green eyeshades and dealer's cuffs.

The other players were very helpful. They gave him a sheet of paper on which they had written the hierarchy of poker hands: full house beats flush, flush beats straight, straight beats three-of-a-kind, etc. He was doing real well for a while.

Then, just when all the money was in the pot, he got dealt queen, ten, eight, six, deuce. All the eyeshade guys looked stricken. They clucked sympathetically and explained to him that he had been unfortunate enough to be dealt a mafuffnick, the only hand in poker worse than aces and eights. It required him to forfeit all his money, all the county of Orange's money, all the school districts' money, all the money of the parishioners where he went to church, his firstborn child and his pants.

The county had to declare bankruptcy. And lack of pants. Bad luck, eh?

The controller's plea was profound ignorance — Ignorance of Previously Unplumbed Depths — which, paradoxically, rose to the level of insanity. I think that's how it went. I can't remember exactly what his punishment was, but I remember thinking it was enlightened, humane and would not cause him to miss any of his favorite soaps.

This is what Jesse Bogdonoff should plead. Yeah, I know it's a civil suit, but what better evidence that our boy Jesse has been *non compos mentis* through all this than if he shows up in his jester's suit and responds to a civil suit with a plea of not guilty by reason of insanity?

The only flaw in this plan is that Tonga probably has stronger evidence than Jesse of mental incapacity. I mean, Tonga invented the job of court jester/financial adviser for him. That alone should suggest its national driveway doesn't reach all the way to the proverbial street. If I were a criminal lawyer with a client who had done anything as crazy as that, I'd probably advise him that he was clearly immune from execution under the Supreme Court's *Atkins v. Virginia* decision.

So I see this as a contest in which some poor trier of fact is going to be confronted with two parties who obviously have trouble keeping both oars in the water and is going to have to figure out which one to throw out of the boat. It's going to be complicated by the fact one is wearing a king uniform and the other is wearing a jester's hat and a Rolex. All in all, it sounds like "Monty Python" meets "The Weakest Link."

Too bad Bob Gardner is body surfing in Corona del Mar these days. He's always been good at picking out weak links. And he knows how to laugh. Whoever tries this case will have to do both. ❖

— November 2002

Save the Dana Point Six

Twenty miles from Disneyland, the Mouseketeers are saddling up again

Here's what it said in the Los Angeles Times, a newspaper which picks up Pulitzers like they were packs of gum at the checkout stand — a newspaper which we can therefore presume did not make this up. It said: "The last time federal wildlife biologists tried to gauge the Pacific pocket mouse population at the Dana Point Headlands, they counted only six of the endangered rodents. However, more than 24 acres of ocean-view real estate — worth $30 million — is being set aside for their protection."

I'll pause here while you re-read that a couple of times. I know you're gonna want to re-read it because it can't really say that, can it? Go ahead, I'll wait.

Yep. That's what it says. Twenty-four acres of ocean-view real estate worth 30 million dollars. For six mice.

Every slander you ever spoke about California — every slur, every joke, every out-and-out calumny — pales in comparison to what really goes on here. It's the world's largest open-air insane asylum, and I am proud to be an inmate.

The Dana Point Headlands is a collection of bluffs above the Pacific Ocean a couple of miles south of my home. A developer wants to clothe them in wood, glass, and stucco. The original developer — God — somehow omitted to provide for human occupation of the Headlands. She covered the land with rocks and trees and grass and mice, but inexplicably forgot houses and hotels and tennis courts. Go figure.

Headlands Reserve LLC wants to correct this oversight. Specifically, it wants to "create 125 lots for custom ocean-view homes, a 65-room seaside inn and commercial development on the 121 acres." But doing so threatens to displace Manny, Moe, Jack, Fred, Ethel, and Britney.[1] This has incurred the wrath of the California animal rights lobby, which is slightly smaller than the National Rifle Association, but equally powerful, much louder, and unencumbered by Charlton Heston.

The upshot will be a battle that will doubtless make Armageddon look like a badminton match. Both sides will bring in platoons of lawyers and spend trashbags full of money. If I weren't otherwise employed — almost gainfully — I would go to every hearing, read every motion, and photograph every demonstration.

Because this is gonna be a classic, folks. This is gonna be *Rome v. Carthage, Grant v. Lee, Ali v. Frazier, Tonya Harding v. Paula Jones*. Even by the comically distorted standards of California, where we've raised wretched excess to an art form, this is an A-list attraction. Trust me, *Rich and Powerful Developers, Inc. v. Six Endangered Little Mice* is gonna be an opinion you'll want to read.

My problem is I'm not sure who to root for. This is nothing new to me. I am a political moderate. I was passed over for appointment by one governor (Jerry Brown, remember him?) because I was too conservative and the next one (George Deukmejian, slightly to the right of Genghis Khan) because I was too liberal. I have a hard time figuring out whether I'm a conservative Democrat or a liberal Republican, but I figure it doesn't much matter because neither label receives anything but scorn and ridicule from the rest of its party.[2]

So it should come as no surprise to me to find myself between Scylla and Charybdis in the latest political crisis to rear its ugly head over my breakfast cornflakes. I don't know why I even read the political news anymore; all it does is make my stomach hurt.

Nonetheless, the ecological catastrophe looming before us as I write this tests even my finely honed ability to face ambivalence with

---

[1] - These aren't really the names of the mice. I made them up. I had to. If I used their real names, I would be violating the Federal Rodent Privacy Protection Act (27 USC 1492).

[2] - And I don't need any more scorn and ridicule, thank you very much; I have a teenage daughter.

equanimity.[3] This one's so confused it's not a matter of separating wheat from chaff, it's a matter of finding the damned farm.

Let me preface this by saying that ecological issues are always tough for me. I'm kind of a conservative conservationist, an alliterative oxymoron which means I usually have one foot in quicksand and the other on ice when these issues come up. If you were a polisci major you'd call me a "boll-weevil" or "mugwump" ecologist, but you'd probably be immediately embarrassed at having sounded like such a nerd.

I'm the type of guy who would horsewhip a man for being cruel to a dog. I get misty if I hear the word "Flicka." My children will never see "Old Yeller" or "Pharlap" if they have to rely on me to pick it up at the video store because my tear ducts couldn't handle seeing either movie again.

You wanna know what a sucker I am for animals? We had a cat who used to bring mice — live mice, endangered mice for all I know — into the house to play with. Every night he'd go out, catch a field mouse, carry it back in through the cat door and turn the family room into a feline thunderdome.

Not only could I not bring myself to lock the furshlugginer cat in or out, I couldn't bring myself to kill the muppergluffing mice! I'd make the cat give them up, then I'd chase them around the house for 20 minutes or so[4], then I'd box them up and drive them to a nearby park and turn them loose! I mean, how animal-whipped can you get?

But I also know people need places to live, which means filling open spaces with houses and displacing animals to build them. While I'll fight to save whales and redwoods, I wouldn't stop the TVA for a snail-darter, and I'm not wholly convinced we need 26 species of goldenrod.

So when I read that we're setting aside four acres PER MOUSE to make sure that *Perognathus longimembris pacificus*[5] shall not perish from the earth, I get a little nervous. I begin to picture all those folks in Alabama and Nebraska and New Jersey laughing at us again.

---

3 - I don't know what the hell that sentence means, either, but gawdam it sounds good, doesn't it?

4 - *That* was worth the price of admission.

5 - Latin for "long-tailed furry creature with a pronounced overbite and ocean-view property."

I don't really mind being the lunatic fringe, you understand, I just hate demonstrating it diurnally.

Please understand, I've got nothing against these mice. We have a lottery in California, which in its entire 12-year history has never been won by anyone as deserving as me, but I've yet to give in to my weekly desire to strangle the unworthy winner. I'm certainly not going to begrudge Manny, Moe, Jack, Fred, Ethel and Britney their chance to be the happiest mice since Mickey.

I mean, these are cute, cuddly little mice. I have no desire to throw six "small, silky mammals with fur-lined cheek pouches" out in the cold.[6] But neither do I understand why we have to make them land barons, for crying out loud.

Four acres! The Times has a picture of one of these cute little critters and the description next to it says it weighs 4-6 ounces. I weigh 210 pounds. That means giving a mouse four acres of prime beachfront property is the equivalent of giving me about a square mile of the stuff. I could put Graceland on that much space and still have room to invite people over for dirt-biking on the weekends.[7] What are the mice gonna do with a lot that big?

The developer who's being forced to give up the acreage thinks they're gonna build little mouse estates on it. Sanford Edwards is quoted by the Times as lamenting, "This mouse basically is going to be living on a nicer lot than me."

A spokesman for the Building Industry Association of Southern California[8] adds, somewhat bemusedly, "That doesn't make much sense. Doesn't it seem like moving them is a much more logical option than preserving that much land for them."

Obviously, this guy knows nothing about the Trail of Tears. Can't you just imagine troops showing up on Pacific Coast Highway to round up six field mice and march them off to Oklahoma to their new reservation? I mean, I'm no James Carville, but I'm pretty sure this

---

6 - Well . . . maybe Britney. But she's the only one. Honest.

7 - Thus reducing the strain on more sensitive environmental areas. What a prince of a guy I am.

8 - These are the developers. They will be wearing the black hats when Hollywood turns this into a movie. Their spokesman will be played by one of the monsters from the movie Alien. Britney the Mouse will be played by Meg Ryan.

is not a politically viable alternative.

Nor can we just write them off on the basis that we have plenty of other Pacific pocket mice. Turns out we've got about a thousand of them a few miles away on the Camp Pendleton Marine Base, but it's been decided that tiny creatures who share land with tanks and fighter planes are even more endangered than those who share it with bulldozers and rich people. So that plan's been scrubbed, too.

As near as I can determine, my personal solution — put the little buggers in a box, carry them to a local park, turn them loose, sell the 24 acres and use the $30 million to house endangered homeless people — is not being considered. Apparently predation by a housecat gets you federal protection, but predation by disease, exposure, hunger, alcoholism, drug abuse and a heartless society gets you a yawn.

We need to come up with something quick. According to the *Times,* "The population is small enough that the mice could be inbreeding, a threat to their future health."

Inbreeding? Nah, they wouldn't do that. Would they?

Seriously, I don't know how many scientists it took to figure out that a population of six mice "could be inbreeding." I'm really hoping the taxes I paid last year weren't earmarked for the study of what a population of six mice might be doing when they aren't eating. But I know trouble when I see it, and a "threat to the future health" of six mice we've apparently decided to protect with a devotion previously reserved for ex-Presidents . . . that's trouble.

Figure it out, folks. Six inbreeding mice means little mouse birth defects and lifelong[9] care in little mouse nursing facilities. It means huge government payouts for mouse drugs and mouse surgeries. Eventually, inevitably, it means lawsuits charging government neglect and inadequate care.

And, since it's California, it means all this ends up in the Ninth Circuit U.S. Court of Appeals: the funhouse mirror of the federal judicial amusement park. The Supreme Court will be so busy reversing mouse cases, it won't have time for anything else. The entire judicial system will boggle to a halt and we'll all have to get real jobs.[10]

---

9 - How long does a mouse live, anyway? I mean if they don't have me to rescue them from the cat and chauffeur them to the park every night?

So I, as a dedicated public servant, offer this modest proposal. Bring 'em over to my house. They can stay in the guest room for a week while I arrange an unfortunate accident. This being southern California, it'll probably take no time at all for them to be gunned down in a drive-by shooting. The mice will — tragically — all be killed in a hail of bullets. There will be much weeping and gnashing of teeth. People will be really upset.

For about an hour.

Then "Friends" will come on and all will be forgotten. The Dana Point Headlands will add 60 half-acre homesites to its present development plan, and this majestic site will be populated as God meant it to be: Not by insignificant little mice, but by developers ... movie stars ... major league third basemen ... former Enron executives ... young women with large breasts whose elderly late husbands died even more tragically than the mice.

And one judge. ❖

— July 2002

---

10 - All right, I've truncated the analysis a little bit here. I was running out of words and didn't have space for a full explication of how the United States Supreme Court closing down would have any effect whatsoever on the rest of us. As you can imagine, that takes a lot of explaining.

Post Post-Impressionist Impressions

Dealing with questions of statuary interpretation

Way, way high up on the disconcertingly long list of Things I Know Nothing About, you will find the entry "art." I am an unregenerate Philistine. If I had been the Nazi general in charge of looting Russia, all those priceless art treasures would have been safe. I would have been the guy shouting, "Forget the Chagalls and the Falconets, grab those doll-within-a-doll-within-a-doll things; those are valuable."

This is an embarrassing admission for me.[1] I've tried to remedy it. I've gone to museums in a dozen cities in four countries. I took a course in art appreciation in college,[2] and I watch Sister Wendy with the kind of fervent single-mindedness with which other men ogle Britney Spears. But it all goes right over my head.

I acknowledge this freely, despite the aforementioned embarrass-

---

1 - Which is saying something. Keep in mind, I admit to working for the National Hockey League, listening to country music, rooting for the California Angels and living in Orange County. It obviously takes a lot to embarrass me.

2 - Yes, it is true that all of us on the baseball tam took the course, but I was awake. Mostly.

ment. Question my understanding of *Advanced Micro Devices. v. Intel* and I'll cross swords with you; question my understanding of Modigliani and I'll signal my corner man to throw in the towel.[3]

Oh, I know a little. I can distinguish a plein air from an airplane. And, given enough time — and a bag of M&M's — I can name most of the primary colors. But for the most part, good art and bad detentions are equally unrecognizable to me.

Sculpture I find especially impenetrable.[4] This is odd since, as a child in the California public school system, my early education consisted almost entirely of being plopped down at a table with a lump of clay and told to make ashtrays.[5]

But it's true. I know Giacometti did the anorexics and Bufano did the zaftigs and Noguchi rolls rocks together, but beyond that I'm lost. If the art world is terra incognita to me, sculpture is the surface of Mercury.

Fortunately, I recognize my limitations in this area. This distinguishes me from, say, the Wisconsin Bar Association. It seems to have made the mistake of thinking it knows something about art. About sculpture, in fact.

According to The Associated Press, the bar association commissioned one David Wanner "to sculpt 'Lady Justice,' a classical figure of a blindfolded woman holding a scale, for their office." He did that. He sculpted Lady Justice. For their office.

Topless.

Oops.

People — or at least the bar association's employees — complained. Apparently the fact the clay model of the sculpture included details that any 12-year-old boy would have recognized as breasts had eluded them. The bar association somehow did not understand Lady Justice would be semi-nude. I guess it thought the artist just hadn't finished dressing her at the time he whipped up the model.[6]

---

3 - Or whatever it is fencers do when they find themselves scheduled for a 12-rounder against the second coming of Zorro.

4 - Yeah, I know it's supposed to be impenetrable. I meant figuratively impenetrable.

5 - Which were then passed on to Kathy Lee Gifford for sale in countries that didn't allow sweat shops.

6 - So to speak.

Why do civic organizations do this to themselves? Why do ordinary people get themselves mixed up with artists? It always leads to misunderstanding. Artists are just way smarter than the rest of us. That's why they can see things in their art the rest of us can't see.

Think about it. You paint the side of your house red, you get a nasty letter from your homeowners association threatening to haul you into court if you don't return it to its original Navajo White or Tampico Tan or whatever within 24 hours. Diego Rivera paints the side of his house red, he sells it for $2 million, buys a new house, and hires a bunch of minimum wage guys to paint the whole thing red before the party he's hosting for the mayor and Bill Gates.[7]

I don't know why this happens. But it does. Let's face fact: Artists are endowed with gray matter not apportioned to the rest of us.[8]

Buffalo learned that before Wisconsin did. In 1992, a civic sculpture for downtown Buffalo was commissioned. No one specified what it should look like. This amazes me. If they'd been buying a garbage truck, they would have delineated every detail right down to the color of the seat covers. But for a major piece of artwork, they just wrote the sculptor a check and went back to shoveling snow.

They ended up in a lawsuit. The artist sued them when they dismantled — rather hastily — "Green Lightning," his statuary portrayal of seven dancing neon penises in top hats. Honest. Whatever you think of me, surely you don't think I could make up seven dancing neon penises in top hats.

The city left the statuary up for five days. Then they had it hauled away. I'm sure they felt a certain urgency about their decision. I mean, just how long can you expect the youth of a city to be exposed to something like this without ... uh, without ... well, without doing whatever it is dancing neon penises in top hats incite.

The jury[9] didn't see it that way, though. The jurors agreed the

---

7 - Yes, yes, I am aware that if Diego Rivera paints his house red, Geraldo Rivera will be there to report on it, since Diego died in 1957. I'm speaking metaphorically here. Try to keep up.

8 - Certain more than Attorney General Ashcroft, a 60-year-old man with a law degree who reported himself astonished to learn that Lady Justice has breasts. As I understand it, he ordered her, "Cover yourself, woman!"

9 - Wouldn't you have loved to hear this case? I'll bet there wasn't a single prospective juror who claimed hardship.

sculptor's rights were violated by the disassembly of his work, but they were unconvinced the sculpture had been damaged.[10]

They also rejected the sculptor's plea for damages for emotional distress. I think they probably got that one right. I just somehow suspect this is a man whose emotions are not easily distressed. If someone with no money is "judgment-proof," I think it can be safely said that someone who constructs sculptures of dancing neon penises in top hats is "emotional distress-proof."

He did prevail, however, in his argument that his freedom of expression had been violated when "Green Lightning" was unbuilt. Another triumph for the First Amendment.

I don't know about you, but I'm pretty sure this is what Thomas Jefferson and James Madison had in mind when they and their rowdy friends wrote the Bill of Rights. While I recognize that there will be a few constitutional scholars who will cavil that there is not a scintilla of evidence to indicate that anyone — in the entire 225 years of this country's existence — had ever previously thought about dancing neon penises in top hats, I am sure the founding fathers — and mothers — would have meant for the First Amendment to protect it.[11]

That's probably what motivated the folks in Wisconsin to reach an early settlement in their dispute. With the Buffalo case as precedent, the bar association must have known it was overmatched. I mean, if Buffalo loses on First Amendment grounds to dancing neon penises in top hats, you gotta figure Wisconsin, having given preliminary approval to the half-clad clay model of Gypsy Rose Justice, had no chance of prevailing in any lawsuit involving the statue.

So the bar association compromised. According to AP, the sculptor "agreed to put a shirt on the statue."

Honest. I'm having as much trouble writing this column as you are believing it, but it's true. That's what it says. "A shirt." The members somehow talked the artist into putting a shirt on his statue.

I don't know whether this is a chambray work shirt or a Grateful

---

10 - This must have been an interesting issue. What would you look for? A dent? A bruise?

11 - Remember, Jefferson is the guy who coined the phrase "pursuit of happiness" and later cut holes in his floors so that his clocks would fit. There's just no telling what he may been thinking.

Dead tie-dye or a recasting of the statue to include buttons and a collar, but whatever it is, I don't like it. I don't know much about art, but I find this "solution" wholly unsatisfying. Next they'll be putting prosthetics and a fielder's glove on the Venus de Milo for fear of offending amputees.

I think you tell the bar association employees to get over it. Lady Justice wears a blindfold, why can't they?

Either that or you give the guy back his sculpture, tell him to resell it to someone whose sensitivities are more in line with those of grown up human beings, and you commission a new one of Oliver Wendell Holmes — with or without shirt. You don't ask the artist to put eyebrows on the Mona Lisa.[12]

But Wisconsin did. Its bar association is now the proud owner of "Lady Justice in a Shirt." Now there's a roadside attraction that oughta stop traffic in Badgerland.

Me, I think I'll take a pass on this one. I'll be too busy trying to find gym shorts to fit Michelangelo's David. ❖

— March 2002

---

12 - No she does not. Get hold of a copy and look at it.

When Pigs Fly

Who says the government is callous?

Even my best-laid plans "gang aft agley."[1] I sat down fully expecting to read two articles in my local legal newspaper: one having to do with the application of Article II of the United States Constitution to the states' selection of presidential electors, and one which promised the explication of Code of Civil Procedure Section 639 pertaining to special references. It was not 30 minutes I expected to rival sex on a beach, but I thought it would be edifying and responsible. Time well spent.

Then my eye was caught by another story. My understanding is that newspapers employ people whose sole task is to write headlines that will catch the eye of innocents like me. Well, this headline writer deserves a raise.

I mean, I was all set to hunker down and open my mind to the vagaries of special masters and referees and whatever the hell the founding fathers had in mind with this electoral college thing, when my eyes fairly leaped across the page to the words, "Flying Pig Wins Approval from FAA." I submit to you that it is impossible to read

---

1- Robert Burns: "The best laid plans o' mice 'n' men gang aft agley."
That concludes the redeeming social value portion of today's column.

anything else once you know there is exposition of words as dumb-founding as those somewhere nearby.

My first thought was that I had misread the headline. "Frying Pigs," "Flying Jibs," "Frigging Pies," almost anything made more sense than that the FAA had somehow approved pigs for flight.

Maybe it wasn't the FAA at all, but the FFA. That would still leave me without explanation for the inexplicable and somewhat unnerving phrase "Flying Pigs," but at least it would be a problem confronting the Future Farmers of America, an organization which — as far as I know — has no effect on the safety of my air travel.

But it clearly said "Flying Pigs," and it clearly said "FAA." There were only two possible explanations for that headline: Either the local legal paper employed a headline writer who would sink so low as to flat out make something up just to keep me from reading scholarly legal articles[2], or the FAA had somehow come out in favor of airborne pork.

My instinct was to blame the headline writer. I once came back from a two-week vacation in Canada to find headlines about a ruling I was supposed to have made three days earlier. This was pretty remarkable to me, since I could remember that day vividly (the fan belt had broken on the rental car) and I was confident I had not taken time out in British Columbia to issue any rulings involving Orange County's most litigious jail inmate, as the newspaper headline fairly shouted I had.

Turned out a federal judge had come down from Mt. Olympus and used my vacant courtroom to hold a hearing on inmate rights. The reporter saw a judge on the bench and a name on the door and connected the dots. I spent months explaining to people that I had most assuredly not ordered the sheriff to pay damages to Bobby Crane for the Playboy magazines confiscated from his cell.

Of course, most of those people knew I was lying because they had read all about it in the newspaper. It was in the headlines, for crying out loud.

But while the headline writer was my most likely suspect, I was not ready to reject out of hand the rather pedestrian notion that a federal bureaucracy could have done something crazy. I carry no brief for bureaucrats, whom I regard as the governmental equivalent of

---

2 - Which would be a pretty good working definition of the word "overkill."

Post-It notes: absolutely necessary, but not to be entrusted with anything important.

Czar Nicholas I is supposed to have said, "I don't rule Russia; ten thousand clerks do." I've dealt with many of those same clerks at the DMV — older now, but still speaking only Russian as near as I can determine. Porcine flight was probably well within the Weltanschauung[3] of the DMV, and, by extension, the FAA. So I was prepared to accept exoneration of the headline writer in favor of a finding of bureaucratic fiasco.

But one way or the other, I couldn't leave it unresolved. I came to the conclusion that I must, reluctantly, postpone Article II and CCP Section 639 and read the four column inches of Associated Press copy regarding the pigs.

Of course, reading anything about the law is — as you probably have surmised on more than one occasion — contrary to the oath taken by all judges. At the black mass conducted by the governor immediately before the announcement of our appointments, we all have to swear that we will never read anything ever again that doesn't involve a box score or Tiger Woods. As I understand it, the family law judges in San Diego actually included that in their Rules of Court, and required special notification if the attorneys expected their files to be read.[4]

But I digress. Here's what the article said. It said, "US Airways acted reasonably when it allowed a pig to fly first class from Philadelphia to Seattle, the Federal Aviation Administration found."

All right, that assuaged my worst fears. No one was hallucinating pigs with wings here. The issue was whether it was kosher for a pig to fly first class.[5]

Here's what happened. "Maria Tirotta Andrews brought Charlotte,

---

3 - Yeah, I know it's pretentious. But it's a really cool word I'd like to see used more often, and if I don't start, who will? Matt Drudge? Dr. Laura?

4 - In which case, a referee would be appointed under CCP Section 639 to read the papers and report back to the judge. (*Lammers v. Superior Court,* (2000) 83 Cal.App.4th 1309.)

5 - I suppose I should rewrite that sentence, since, strictly speaking, it's probably not "kosher" for a pig to do anything, but rewrites are another thing forbidden in the black mass oath for judges. That should explain your last 10 petitions for rehearing.

her 300-pound Vietnamese potbellied[6] pig, on the flight Oct. 17, telling the airline it was a "therapeutic companion pet." Andrews said her heart condition was so severe she needed the pig to relieve stress."

That's what she said. She said taking a 300-pound pig on an airplane would relieve her stress. Honest. I don't know, I suppose setting fire to the clerk's office would relieve my stress, but it never occurred to me I could get a federal agency to sign off on that.

See, I would have gotten this question wrong. If this question had shown up on my FAA Bureaucrat Qualification Examination, I would have narrowed the list of possible answers down to either "C. You gotta be kidding." or "D. Take the lady and the pig up to about 30,000 feet and then throw them both overboard." I like to think I would have chosen "C" but it would have been a tough call, and I can get pretty grumpy when I have to make a decision, so I can't guarantee anything here.

I suppose this is why nobody's breaking down the doors to get me to do alternative dispute resolution. I'm obviously not sensitive enough to the problems of modern life.

I mean, I've had dogs and cats I have loved dearly. I had a contraband guinea pig in my apartment the whole time I was going to law school, and I cried when he died. I love animals so much I watch the credits after the movie to make sure "no animals were harmed in the filming of this feature." Even if it's a cartoon.

But I'm not gonna let the lady take her pig on the airplane. She's lucky she had the FAA calling this one and not me.

After all, this is a THREE HUNDRED POUND PIG.[7] Imagine that. THREE HUNDRED POUNDS. This is not some terrier-sized shoat. A THREE HUNDRED POUND PIG is roughly the size of

---

6 - Do we really need the adjective "potbellied" to describe a 300-pound pig? Aren't we pretty much gonna come up with that picture anyway? I think until they breed a "Vietnamese Washboard-Stomached Pig" or a "Vietnamese Incredibly-Buff Pig," we don't really need an adjective here.

7 - It occurs to me — as I'm sure it occurred to the other passengers — that only capital letters adequately convey the notion of a THREE HUNDRED POUND PIG, and therefore I will use that font hereinafter. (The black mass oath requires that we use the word hereinafter a lot; I've been remiss.)

Shaquille O'Neal. And not nearly as well-dressed.

If you had a three hundred pound human being in the seat next to you you'd want your money back. How you gonna feel about a THREE HUNDRED POUND PIG?!

It seems to me it contradicts the whole notion of "first class" if there's a THREE HUNDRED POUND PIG in it. What about all those other passengers who paid for first class? Didn't they have an implied agreement with the airline that they would not be sitting with farm animals?

And just what is it this pig is going to do for Ms. Andrews' heart condition? Is the pig's name DeBakey? Is the pig a licensed psychotherapist? Did the pig take an oath the night before his appointment as a "therapeutic companion pet" to soothe people with heart conditions?[8]

Because if he[9] did, he clearly violated it upon landing. That's how this thing got to the FAA. Seems the other passengers objected, not when the pig took his seat next to Ms. Andrews,[10] but when "the pig got unruly when the plane landed." These people not only deserved a refund, but an award for forbearance.

I think they had a legitimate complaint. I think when you pay $1,200 for a first-class ticket, you deserve not to become the headliner in a WWF pig-wrestle. If the lady wants to bring on her golden retriever or her cat Snowball, fine. If she wants to bring on Mount St. Helens the Pig, you gotta draw the line.

Let me hasten to point out here that this is not special pleading. I have never in my whole life flown first-class. But I will if they start flying pigs in coach.

I would have expected the FAA to be able to understand that. Hell, I would have expected the Executive Committee of the Kona Lanes Midnight Tuesday Turkey Bowl League to have understood it.

But apparently I gave the FAA too much credit. I think next time I wanna go to their black mass. ❖

---

8 - Which, as you've already guessed, is the opposite of the one judges take at the black mass.

9 - I'm pretty sure you're allowed to use male pronouns if you're referring to pigs.

10 - These were passengers who gave new meaning to the phrase "latter day saints."

Fat-Busted

There's trouble in paradise for a popular weight loss plan

H.L. Mencken was a journalist, editor and all-around iconoclast who wrote for Baltimore newspapers in the first half of the last century.[1] He wrote clear, intelligent, devastating prose, but by most accounts that was his only redeeming social value.

He was apparently not a warm human being. He was the type of man who goes through life agnostic because he cannot conceive of a deity stupid enough to put him on a planet full of abysmally inferior beings. His idea of a good breakfast was three puppies and a can of Sterno.

And he was not a big fan of the legal profession. He once wrote that, "If all lawyers were hanged tomorrow, and their bones sold to a mah jongg factory, we'd be freer and safer and our taxes would be reduced by almost half."

We've all known people like Mencken. We've all appeared before people like Mencken: Judges who go through life like they're Grant at Vicksburg and their big decision for the day is going to be whether they'd get greater enjoyment out of laying seige to you and watching

---

1- The "H. L." stands for "Henry Louis." I figure with the footnote this sentence qualifies for MCLE credit. So this time you actually will get something out of reading my column.

you starve to death, or whether they should just shoot your little gray ass and move the army east.

But Mencken was not all bad. He correctly identified New York as a "third-rate Babylon," and he left behind a legacy of writing so good that reading 10 pages of it guarantees that your own next three sentences will be more concise.

He also penned an epigram which is as accurate today, 70 years after he wrote it, as it was then, an observation so preternaturally apropos that it is usually referred to simply by the shorthand reference, "Mencken was right."

What he said was, "No one ever went broke underestimating the intelligence of the American people."

I was reminded of this today when I read, "The marketers of a weight-loss system that claimed to block fat and burn calories without exercise agreed Wednesday to repay $10 million to customers to settle government charges that they used deceptive advertising."

You may have seen the infomercials for this one. It's called the Enforma System, and it consists of two products: "Exercise in a Bottle" and the "Fat-Trapper." According to the FTC, the ads in question ran 30,000 times.

Now I don't know about you, but it seems to me the FTC shouldn't have needed 30,000 viewings to know that something called the "Fat-Trapper" might merit scrutiny. Thirty thousand times in 10 months works out to about 100 times a day they ran this thirty-minute infomercial. That's 900,000 minutes. That seems to me like 899,999 minutes more than it should have taken to set off the smoke alarms.

Even allowing for the fact that most of those showings were on cable between one and four in the morning, I would have thought the FTC would have one insomniac who would have said, "You know, 'Exercise in a Bottle' sounds more like something cooked up in the bathtub at a frat house than a medical breakthrough; maybe we oughta look into this." If I'd been the FTC, I woulda been on it like a duck on a junebug.

I suspect the reason they were so slow in responding was that the infomercial for "Fat-Trapper" and "Exercise in a Bottle" featured Steve Garvey, the erstwhile first baseman for the Los Angeles Dodgers and San Diego Padres. I'm sure it was hard for them to imagine the lantern-jawed ex-Michigan State d-back, who tours the motivational speaking circuit lecturing on "The Rewards of Living a Christian Life," would be involved in anything that wasn't on the square.

Garvey, you might recall, once told Playboy magazine, "Running for the U. S. Senate is an option I would hopefully have at the end of my professional baseball career. ... I wouldn't have time for local politics. I start at the U.S. Senate or nothing." Then his life turned into a Sally Jessy Raphael episode, and he apparently decided conquering obesity would be easier than dealing with Sam Donaldson.

All of which brings me to my own corollary of Mencken's Law, which is: "No enterprise which takes advantage of the tendency of the American people to act like star-struck morons will ever fail."[2] For reasons I've never been able to fathom, our citizenry proves me right and Darwin wrong every time the slightest hint of celebrity is involved. If you can throw a ball, have sex with a president, or marry a stranger on TV, we will throw so much money and attention at you that your safety will be endangered.

And your wallet fattened.

And if you've ever done anything that extended your allotted 15 minutes of fame past the Warhol limit, you are presumed to speak the gospel. The American people will believe anything said by anyone they've ever seen on TV.[3]

So the Garvey commercials featured Steve telling us, "I've always been an athlete, and I know what exercise can do for the body." Then having extolled the wonders of exercise, he proceeded to tell us to forget exercise; we could eat all the cheeseburgers, sausage pizza and chocolate cake we wanted, as long as we swallowed enough "Exercise in a Bottle" and "Fat-Trapper" pills — at $70 for a two-month supply.

And you know what? We bought it.

We bought carloads of it. The Enforma people say they have more than a million customers. More than a MILLION! That's why they're so willing to disgorge $10 million in the FTC settlement. That's chump change to them — in the most literal meaning of the term.

Now in fairness to all us sheep, Garvey made this stuff pretty irre-

---

2 - Yeah, I know. Not as memorable as Mencken's. Pith is not my forte.

3 - With the possible exception of Janet Reno who, for reasons I've never understood, doesn't seem ever to convince anyone of anything.

sistible. Not only did he smile that great celebrity smile — my God, the man's got more teeth than an Osmond — but he threw in what must have seemed irresistible lagniappe at 3 a.m.: If you were one of the first people to call after the infomercial, you received — absolutely free of charge — the Enforma Pill Carrying Case.

As near as I can determine this was a plastic container in which to carry your pills. Apparently if you weren't one of the lucky first callers, you didn't get a container for your pills. Apparently, the pills were brought to your home by a surly Fed-Ex guy who took them out of a sack and threw them — at you one by one.

And, of course, if you were one of the lucky first callers, you also received — also free of charge[4] — the Enforma System Guide to Sensible Eating.

Now, I have not read the Enforma System Guide to Sensible Eating. My job requires a lot of reading, and it's hard to find time to squeeze in The Hockey News and Robert Parker, much less the ESGSE. But I have a pretty good idea what it says. I'm convinced it says you can't lose weight unless you eat less food.

I'm convinced it must say this because I know it to be true. That's why I myself am so big my shadow leaves marks on the pavement. If there were pills to make you skinny, I would not be within five pounds of qualifying for my own zip code.

And the Enforma people agree. Their president, one Andrew Grey, says they'll be happy to accede to the FTC's order that Enforma "include in its packaging and ads the statement that 'reduced caloric intake is required to lose weight.'" Grey says they "will gladly do that because we believe that."[5]

So I'm sure that's what's in the Enforma System Guide to Sensible Eating.

And I'm sure that I must have misunderstood Steve Garvey when I thought he was suggesting I could eat Cleveland without noticeable effect, so long as I took his pills. I think the FTC must have misconstrued the ads when it said that "Enforma promoted the pills in a way

---

4 - Does the phrase "ginsu knife" suggest itself to you yet?

5 - And, Enforma's attorney, Edward Glynn, whose thought processes are so similar to Grey's it makes you wonder if they were separated at birth, says payment of the $10 million under the FTC order "simply extends the company's tradition of offering a money-back guarantee." Now there's a guy Mencken would have loved. Also P. T. Barnum.

that told people they could eat whatever high-fat food they want."

Because if they really did that ... if they really told a MILLION people, at $70 per two-month supply, that they "could eat whatever high-fat food they wanted" and lose weight, $10 million doesn't sound like a lot. And the FTC apparently recognizes that because they told the Washington Post the money would be refunded to consumers who purchased the products, and — this is the part I like — "If there are too many consumers demanding redress and not enough money to go around, however, the $10 million may go into the U. S. Treasury."

So Washington gets the $10 million (for a bridge in the district of some otherwise unelectable congressperson), Steve Garvey and Enforma attorney Edward Glynn get fees big enough to bloat a horse (if the horse weren't taking "Fat-Trappers"), and Enforma makes a bloody fortune. And the consumers get ... left holding the empty Enforma Pill Carrying Case.

Mencken was right. ❖

— June 2000

Who Moved My Woolsack?

The ancient post of Lord High Chancellor bites the dust before the queen can call

In a classic case of "You snooze, you lose," I seem to have missed out on my chance to become Lord High Chancellor of Great Britain. This is what happens when you don't keep up with the job market in your chosen field.

I've been considering a job change for a long time. I'm pretty much topped-out in my present occupation. I talked to Chief Justice George about it, and he confirmed that there are no courts higher than my own whose windows require daily washing.

So I was thinking outside the box that is the California judiciary. The chief had suggested Senegal and East Timor as countries with a high incidence of dirty glass. And after I wrote *Wiener v. Southcoast Childcare Centers Inc.,* (2003) 107 Cal.App.4th 1429, Justice Sills generously offered to underwrite my moving expenses.

But both jobs seemed likely to require language skills and malarial immunity that I have not yet developed, so I had given up on them and wasn't actively looking for work. Unfortunately, despite the remarkably high number of people who've told me lately that I missed my calling, none had suggested the Lord High Chancellor position.

And now it's gone. Great Britain has abolished the post and replaced it with a Department for Constitutional Affairs. While this would seem auspicious news indeed — given the British penchant for governmental sex scandals, an entire department devoted to governmental affairs seems on its face to be an idea fairly brimming with both self-insight and entertainment value — the term "affairs" turns out not to relate to Clintonesque matters at all, but only to "things pertaining to the judiciary." This is a crushing disappointment to those of us with both a proper regard for British tradition and a well-honed appreciation of the salacious.

But it's especially hard on me, since I'm only now finding out that my destiny did not involve tropical climes at all. The job was waiting for me in England, where there are no mosquitoes, and they speak a language I am confident I could learn.

I'm sure I could have gotten the job. I can't believe there were many applicants for it. Maybe that's why they closed it down.

I mean, let's take a quick look at some of the more famous Lord High Chancellors as described by The Associated Press: "Thomas Becket, who became Archbishop of Canterbury and was martyred by King Henry II was a Lord Chancellor. So was Thomas More, executed in 1535 for refusing to recognize Henry VIII as head of the church. Cardinal Wolsey, chancellor to Henry VII and Henry VIII ... died in prison awaiting trial for treason."

That's not a very felicitous history, now is it? I mean, how many people do you think would want to play center field for the Yankees if they had executed Joe DiMaggio and Mickey Mantle, and Bobby Murcer had died in prison.

Granted, if you're into wielding power, this might be an attractive position. Lotta juice in this gig. Near as I can determine, the Lord High Chancellor is like a federal judge on steroids.

"The Lord Chancellor is simultaneously a judge, a legislator and a member of the cabinet." He is the Speaker of the House of Lords, president of the Supreme Court, sits occasionally as a judge in the House of Lords, tells the queen whom to appoint to the bench, plays center-half for Tottenham Hotspur, directs three movies a year and owns a Hallmark shop in Chelsea.

This has caused some griping among sticklers who feel that maybe, as Lord Falconer put it, "the person who appoints judges should not be a member of the executive, a member of the legislature and involved, as well, as the head of the judiciary. Besides, his three-picture-a-year deal is better than Spielberg gets."[1]

I dunno. I think if you got the right guy, the whole separation of powers thing is generally overrated. And, sadly, I was that guy.

I was born to be Lord High Chancellor. According to The Associated Press, the uniform consists of "a flowing, full-bottomed wig, ermine-trimmed robes, breeches, stockings and silver-buckled shoes." This is, of course, one of my better outfits. My silver-buckled shoes are to die for.

Contrast my own personal splendor with that of the unworthy Lord Irvine of Lairg, the outgoing and final Lord High Chancellor. I mean, I don't want to sound catty, but the man is simply unable to pull off the ermine trimmed robes and flowing wig thing. He looks like Jar-Jar Binks in drag.

And he knows it. He actually petitioned parliament to allow him to wear ordinary trousers rather than tights and breeches for his appearances there. I would never have done that. Once they got me into tights and breeches, it would have taken a king's ransom[2] to get me out. Also a full rescue crew employing the Jaws of Life.

I would have been perfect. According to The Associated Press, "During the State Opening of Parliament, the Lord Chancellor delivered the Throne Speech to the monarch to be read aloud. Afterward he descended the stairs to the throne backward so as not to turn his back on his sovereign." I could do this; I can walk backwards.

According to AP, "The Lord Chancellor was guardian of the Great Seal." I love animals.

"The post also served as speaker in the House of Lords, presiding over debates from his seat on the woolsack — a red cushion stuffed with wool gathered from around the Commonwealth." Presiding over debates is my present job description, I own two red cushions, which sit next to my living room fireplace and could be easily shipped to London after we brush the cat hair off them, and I've probably indulged in more woolgathering than any judge in California.

---

1 - I think this was what Lord Falconer said, but I might have gotten it mixed up with something Arnold Schwarzenegger or Cruz Bustamante or Gary Coleman or Rin Tin Tin or one of our other gubernatorial candidates said the other day. These are difficult times in California, and it's not always easy to remember the source of every nonsensical allocution.

2 - A phrase I would have deleted from my vocabulary if I'd gotten the job.

Who better than I?

I even have some good ideas about staffing. "On formal occasions such as the opening of parliament or the Law Courts, the Lord Chancellor is attended by a procession of five persons. First comes a tipstaff; then the official who holds the joint offices of Permanent Secretary to the Lord Chancellor and Clerk of the Crown in Chancery; then the Mace-Bearer; then the Purse-Bearer; then the Lord Chancellor himself, and lastly a Train-Bearer." Obviously, we can't do without the Train-Bearer or the tipstaff[3], but, in the interests of economy and good government, I would have been willing to carry my own purse and mace.[4]

But what really convinces me that this was my destiny is this final paragraph from the AP story: "Lord Irvine ... was appointed in 1997 and spent $1 million on renovations to the House of Lords apartment that came with his job, including $95,000 on wallpaper."

A job with a $95,000 wallpaper allowance? Now that's a cool job.

I worried a little that maybe Lord Irvine had spent his own money on this, but I'm confident that could not be the case. I've done a little research and I'm now quite sure no member of my gender has ever, in the history of the cosmos, spent $95,000 on wallpaper.

As near as I can determine, the previous record was $72,000 by Cardinal Wolsey in 1530. That's why they charged him with treason. And we all know how that turned out.[5]

But I must admit to one reservation about the job. According to R. F. V. Heuston, "A paragraph may be added here about the peculiar concept that the Lord Chancellor is 'keeper of the King's conscience.' Nobody has been clear as to what this phrase, apparently first used by Hatton in 1587, meant." I would be a little reluctant to take on a position whose job description included a role at once so weighty and so undefined.

This may not have been a big problem for Lord Irvine, since I shouldn't think Queen Elizabeth's conscience would be too fractious a colt.

But I'm not sure I want to sign on as "keeper of the conscience"

---

3 - Hell if I know. Look it up; I can't be expected to do everything for you.

4 - Actually, I figure if I'm gonna carry a purse, I probably better have some mace in it. I can't believe they were using two people for this.

5 - At least we do if we've been reading carefully and are ready for tomorrow's quiz.

for any of her likely successors. These look like high-spirited boys, and keeping any of their consciences might require the re-employment of the Mace-Bearer and the Purse-Bearer, as well as several Long-Shoremen, a Line-Backer and a Steer-Wrestler.

It wouldn't do for someone from Orange County to be a Budget-Buster. Maybe I'm better off where I am.

Someday Sills and George will realize my loss was their gain. ❖

— September 2003

Meet Me in St. Louis

Bush v. Gore didn't resolve all our election problems

When I die, I want to move to St. Louis.

This was not an easy decision — especially since the sum total of all my time in St. Louis consists of a Cardinals-Astros game in 1988, during which the temperature and the humidity both exceeded my body temperature. But it appears that St. Louis provides better post-mortem benefits to its citizens than other cities, so I'm thinking that's the place for me.

Most important to me is St. Louis' practice of extending the voting franchise beyond the grave. According to the Los Angeles Times: "At least three dead aldermen registered to vote in Tuesday's mayoral primary. So did one alderman's deceased mother.

"And a dead man was listed as the chief plaintiff in a lawsuit filed on election day in November. He was having trouble voting, the suit said, due to long lines at his polling station. So he petitioned a judge — successfully — to keep city ballot boxes open late."

I think that's tremendously helpful information for someone trying to pick a place to spend the hereafter. The prospect of being interred somewhere that will allow me to continue not only voting, but perhaps practicing on behalf of my fellow dead people appeals to me. I don't want to practice a lot, but it would be nice to have an occasional petition granted, just for old time's sake.

And it would be especially nice to be able to dabble in something as important as voting rights law. You see, my family has a long history of working for voting rights in Missouri, and it would be pleasant to continue that tradition.

My grandmother worked for the Democratic Party in Kansas City when Tom Pendergast ran it like it was his personal cookie jar. Every election day, Grandma would gather up my father and my two uncles — none of whom was old enough to go to a prom, much less vote in an election — and take them from polling place to polling place so they could cast votes on behalf of dead Democrats.[1]

One of my family's favorite stories has to do with the day Grandma's picture showed up on the front page of the Kansas City Star. The caption read something like, "Grace Bedsworth stands in line to be first to vote at her polling place before taking her sons to school."

It was a very nice picture of Grandma and you could make out my dad in the background. Only problem was, it wasn't her polling place. It was just one of the two dozen she and her intrepid three-boy band of electoral facilitators for the dearly departed would hit that day. For weeks, the family lived in fear of having one of their neighbors look at that picture and say, "Hey, what in hell is Grace Bedsworth doing voting way out by Swope Park?"

I'm not saying Harry Truman would not have made it to the Senate without Grandma, but I'm pretty sure the Bedsworths cast more votes for him than any town with a population under 30,000. My father is 82 now and refuses to vote. He says he used up his franchise before he was 15. Says it wouldn't be fair for him to cast any more votes than he already has.

So I'm not surprised to hear St. Louis has such an enlightened policy about extending voting rights to dead people. St. Louis and Kansas City have one of those confused familial relationships that are hard to describe without spending way too much time discussing Luke Skywalker and Darth Vader. Suffice it to say, Dostoevsky

---

1· Grandma was confident she knew how these people would have voted had they not been encumbered by several feet of earth. So it wasn't so much electoral fraud as just assisting the electorally handicapped.

would have understood these people, but nobody else does. All you really gotta know is if Kansas City has dead people voting, then there's no way St. Louis is going to be without it.

Besides, as Grandma always said, it just wouldn't make sense to deny fine, upstanding citizens the right to vote just because they don't happen to be capable of actually upstanding on the day of the election. How arbitrary would that be?

So I guess I'm not too surprised to learn that dead people have the franchise in Missouri, but I must admit I did not previously understand that corpses were allowed access to the state's courts. At the risk of being accused of impermissible group bias, I have to say this seems a little extreme to me.

Turns out St. Louis was one of the cities we heard about last November where there were inexplicable long lines at the polls, and judges were being asked to order polling places to stay open late. And who was asking them to do this? Dead people.

According to the Times, "The lawsuit that won extended voting hours [in St. Louis] was filed on behalf of a Robert Odom. It indicated that he 'has not been able to vote and fears he will not be able to vote' because of crowding at his polling place. It later emerged that Odom had died a year earlier."

Hear that? Not only do dead people vote, but they turn out in such huge numbers that they clog up the system. St. Louis on election day must look like the closing scenes of "Night of the Living Dead." [2]

Actually, I find that a little distressing. You would think people who have been dead for a year would be occupied with weightier thoughts than whether their polling place would be crowded, wouldn't you? This indicates to me that heaven may not be all it's cracked up to be. All the more reason to think seriously about your postmortem domicile.

Now, if you're like me,[3] the question that comes to mind is, just how did the late Mr. Odom get emergency relief in a St. Louis court? How did he make a record? I mean, when I was in a trial court, I re-

---

2 - The phone number of the California secretary of state's office is (916) 653-6814. You will probably want to call Bill Jones and thank him personally for all he's done to keep this from happening in California.

3 - Don't panic: "If you're like me" is a figure of speech, not a request for admissions.

quired at least an affidavit before I'd issue a TRO. Sometimes I took live testimony.

For obvious reasons, this latter option was not available in Mr. Odom's case.[4] So I can only surmise Missouri law allows declarations under penalty of perjury from dead people.

Which makes sense to me. Who has better reason to fear the consequences of violation of an oath than a dead person? I mean, my theology certainly admits of the possibility of someone having his station in the after-life diminished if God finds out he lied under oath. I figure God don't need no stinking extradition treaty. In fact, I doubt that an omniscient God even affords you a hearing for this sort of thing. So I can understand an argument in favor of dead people's affidavits.[5]

But the Times indicates maybe I'm reading a little too much eschatology into this whole thing. Their article suggests there may be less Teilhard de Chardin at issue here and more Richard J. Daley. It says, "The lawyer who filed the suit explained the mix-up by saying he had intended the plaintiff to be Robert 'Mark' Odom, an aide to a Democratic candidate for Congress. But that Odom had voted, without a wait, by the time the suit was filed."

Well, I'm sorry, but that's just not my idea of an "explanation."

Essentially, this guy's "explanation" was, "Hey, you know how it is. We already had this lawsuit all written, and it had lots of 'wherevers' and 'therebys' and even some 'heretofores' in it, and it just looked so purty, that when it turned out our own Mr. Odom had no problem voting, we just didn't have the heart to toss all them fancy papers with all that lawyerly outrage into the trash. And we wuz nearly all outta white-out. So we just used a dead Odom. There's

---

4 - At least not without giving a whole new meaning to the phrase "dead man walking."

5 - And while I'm at it, I should indicate there is some precedent for this sort of thing here in Orange County. My friend Cliff Roberts once had a plaintiff die shortly after filing a complaint on his behalf. Cliff tried to dismiss the complaint, but his motion was rejected by the court clerk's office via a form letter which had a box checked that read, "Affidavit required." So Cliff drew up a document (I have a file-stamped copy before me) that said, "My name is Joe Shlabotnick. I am dead." He attached this to his motion to dismiss, resubmitted it and got his dismissal without further inquiry.

plenty o' them dead folks discouraged by the long lines."[6]

Either the Times is guilty of some pretty shoddy journalism — which I find highly unlikely because I keep a pretty close eye on them and they almost always get the hockey scores right — or some lawyer in Missouri actually "explained" how he filed a suit on behalf of a dead person by saying that the plaintiff turned out not to have had his rights violated, and the only available person WITH THE SAME NAME happened to be dead.

And this caused not the batting of an eyelash in St. Louis. No immediate suspension, no call for disbarment, no investigation into how he got a judge to sign this thing, not even so much as, "You're still using white-out?" Nothing.

What's that? You say your plaintiff has no cause of action, and you've already drawn up the complaint? No problem. Use a dead plaintiff. The cemeteries are full of 'em, and Lord knows, they got nothin' but time. They'll be happy to come to court.

This apparently meets the standard of practice in Missouri. And the general public is way too concerned with the rehabilitation of Mark McGwire's knee to get too caught up in falsified affidavits. Near as I can determine, their attitude is, "Hey, we got all these dead people voting, we gotta make some accommodation to the physical problems that involves. We'll just leave the polls open longer. Hell, the ADA probably requires that."

So look for the polls to be open late in Missouri. But don't look too hard: You're liable to see my grandmother there with a handful of death certificates. ❖

— April 2001

---

6 - Which is surprising, really. You'd think people who do — literally — have an eternity, would be more patient than the rest of us.

Monkey Business Can Be Hard on Monkeys

Even the rally monkey wouldn't be welcome here

I've been doing a lot of traveling lately. I'm on what some people call the Rubber Chicken Circuit. Public-speaking engagements. In the past year, I've traveled to Honolulu, Tulsa, Omaha, New York City, Rapid City, Seattle, San Francisco, Orange Beach, Alabama,[1] Palm Desert and Kona.

This is not natural. People who make all their court appearances don't usually do this much moving around.

But folks in other parts of the country seem to have come up a little short on entertainment this year, and they've decided 30 minutes of listening to a Californian is probably funnier than anything Fox or the WB are liable to come up with.

So they've dangled chicken cordon bleu or chicken cacciatore or chicken teriyaki or whatever combination of dead bird and starch is indigenous to their area, and I have risen to the bait. I've been through almost as many time zones as that home run Barry Bonds hit against Troy Percival in Game 2 of the World Series.

It's been a great deal for Kelly and me. They treat us like royalty.

1- Honest. Turns out Alabama has a coupla hundred yards of Gulf Coast near Pensacola. Who knew?

We get to stay in beautiful hotels, go to dress-up parties,[2] watch the nightly news in strange and exotic places and convince people they were absolutely right about Californians.

Kelly calls it, "Being rich, part time."

I call it, "Slandering an entire state just by being myself."

Because I figure I do enough damage to California's image just by showing up, I work real hard at not adding further embarrassment to that calumny. I turn off my cell phone on the plane. I "remember that the white zone is for loading and unloading of passengers only," and I do not carry monkeys in my underwear.

This last is a fairly recent decision. Not the conduct. That's always been my practice. I've never carried monkeys in my underwear. Honest.

But only recently have I realized there was a decision involved. I don't recall ever making a conscious choice NOT to carry monkeys in my underwear. It just never occurred to me that was an option.

But it is. I know this because, "A man nabbed with two endangered pygmy monkeys in his pants after his flight from Thailand landed at Los Angeles International Airport pleaded guilty Tuesday to smuggling protected wildlife." The Copley News Service says so, and I have no reason to doubt it.

No reason, that is, other than the fact it is hard for me to imagine SHARING MY UNDERWEAR WITH MONKEYS!

Think about this. The man had pygmy monkeys in his underwear. Live ones.

How long does a flight from Thailand to Los Angeles take? Twenty hours? At least that. And it's probably not non-stop. Twenty hours.

Compare that time to the maximum amount of time you would want pygmy monkeys hanging out in your crotch. If the two numbers are within nineteen hours and fifty-nine minutes of each other, I have been defrauding all those people in the other states: You should be the one modeling California nut cake at bar conferences nationwide, not me.

"In entering his plea, Robert John Cusack, 45, of Palm Springs, acknowledged that he carried the monkeys, called lesser slow lorises, in the crotch area of his underwear on a Korean Air flight June 13." The article describes the animals as "endangered" but it is unclear

---

2 - Kelly loves dress-up parties. Me, not so much.

whether lesser slow lorises are endangered in general or only when idiot humans play pocket pool with them.

You know what amazes me about this? The fact that we had to make sharing your shorts with monkeys a crime. The fact the conduct wasn't its own deterrent.

You know what doesn't amaze me? That it was a Californian who did it. I don't know whether our school system's lagging behind or our access to country music is too limited or our ozone layer is letting us down, or what, but it's just becoming harder and harder to maintain even a charade of sanity in the face of evidence like this. It's hard to think up a convincing retort when someone from Mississippi says, "California: That's where they put primates in their package isn't it?"

Well, ... mm ... uh, yes it is.

"Cusack was also found with four endangered birds of paradise and 50 orchids in his luggage." I just don't know what to make of this. I live in a city where 50 orchids wouldn't raise an eyebrow. In Laguna, that's not a crime, it's an outfit.

But the birds of paradise thing turns out to be a little disturbing. These were REAL birds of paradise. They had feathers. One of them escaped and flew around LAX. According to Assistant U.S. Attorney Joseph Johns, the sight of a dozen customs officials chasing a bird of paradise around the Tom Bradley International Terminal "created quite a ruckus."

I suspect that bird may have set the record for MOST endangered bird of paradise in the history of the planet. While I had not previously realized it, there were probably lots of people in the terminal who would gladly have stuffed it into their drawers if given half a chance.

This is really more information than I wanted to have. I'll probably never be able to look at people debarking from international flights again without wondering what wondrous things they have packed in their pants. I think I would have been a lot more comfortable in airports without knowing there were people like Mr. Cusack in the world.

It must be tough to be a customs official. I mean, they must see this kind of aberrance every day. According to the Copley News Service, they detected the lorises "when Cusack was selected for a secondary examination at a U.S. Customs Service station at LAX."

How do you think they "selected" him? You think it was because his genitalia seemed unusually ... active? Can't you just imagine the decision-making process?

"Say, Paul ..."

"Yeah?"

"Take a look at that bloke's crotch.[3]"

"I beg your pardon?"

"No, seriously, that chap right over there. Aren't his jewels a few more carats than most?"

"Why, yes, Cliff, they are. They definitely are. And they seem to be swinging around more than most too."

"Whoa, did you see that? His left testicle just jumped up to his waist. You don't see that very often, now do you? Not even on a flight from Thailand."

"Oops, the right one's started leaping around now. Either this guy's a porn star or he's subletting his Calvin Kleins."

"You think we have to search him?"

"I think YOU have to search him; you're the one that was staring at men's crotches."

According to the article, "Cusack denied having anything hidden on his body." Well, of course he did. This is not exactly the type of crime anybody cops to.

Excuse me, sir, United States Customs. Did you pack your own pants today? Have they been under your control since you packed them? Did anyone give you anything to carry in your underwear? Are there any small primates currently sharing space with your genitalia?"

What are you gonna say? "Well ... you know ... now that you mention it, I dozed off for a few minutes in Kuala Lumpur and since then I've noticed that my briefs seem to have a fur lining that I don't remember noticing before."

No, you just gotta be brazen it out. "Lorises!!! You found lorises in my underwear!? How could that happen!? Dammit, I'm never flying Korean Air again!!"

But by the time you reach arraignment, you should have benefited from the advice of counsel. Trust me on this one. I spent a long time

---

3 - The customs official was originally from New Zealand. It's my hypothetical; I'll give him whatever heritage I choose.

practicing criminal law. Believe me when I tell you there is no non-culpable explanation for monkeys in your underwear. I'm sure counsel advised him to make a clean breast of it.[4]

Under the terms of his plea bargain, he has agreed "to contribute $11,550 as a form of community service" like cleaning up highways or volunteering at a hospital or lecturing school groups. The feds are a lot more pragmatic than we state types: You give $11,550 to the community, that's a service. Hence, "community service." Forget the highways; show us the money.

Cusack's also looking at jail time and a $10,000 fine. I hope he doesn't get jail time. You can imagine where monkey nuzzlers rate in the prison hierarchy. Jail time could be cruelly and unusually unpleasant for this guy.

But my favorite part of the plea agreement is that Cusack must 7"pay $3,450 in restitution." I can only assume that's emotional distress restitution to be paid to the monkeys. Who certainly deserve it.[5]

Me, I'm going to Colorado. Sans lorises. ❖

— December 2002

---

4 - And burn his shorts.

5 - Twenty hours trapped in Goliath's underpants? $3,450 seems way low.

Snow-Blind in Laguna

We need more of the stuff. Or less.

Arlo Guthrie once said, "There's two ways of looking at the drug problem: There's the folks who think there's too much drugs, and there's the folks who think what there is ain't good enough."

That was 30 years ago, and as near as I can determine, we aren't a whole lot closer to resolving our national ambivalence about whether drugs are *malum prohibitum* or *malum in se* than we were when Arlo was singing "The Motorcycle Song," and hanging out at Alice's Restaurant.

Come to think of it, that may have been the problem. The fact the only person who said anything about drugs that I still remember is someone who once made a living out of coming up with three chords to play while intoning, "I don't want a pickle; I just want to ride on my motorcycle[1]," suggests to me that part of our problem is drug czars who overestimated their audience.

At any rate, here we are years later, walking on the moon and conquering polio but unable to reach a consensus on why tobacco and tequila are different from marijuana and mescaline. We can all agree to turn Afghanistan and Iraq into skateboard parks if need be, but we

---

1- And making it *rhyme*.

can't decide who should be allowed to stand next to the pile and inhale while we're burning the weeds.

I find this all very strange, but what I find even stranger is that we completely ignore a substance whose apparent deleterious effect on mental health is inexplicably neglected in medical literature. I've searched in vain for an indication that mainstream medical thought has dealt with this problem, so I've finally decided I'm going to have to take the lead on this.

I haven't worked out all the kinks yet, but I've decided that time is of the essence since ski season is upon us. And I've done enough accumulation of data to be able to postulate the basic hypothesis, so this seems like an appropriate time to set out my initial findings: Snow causes brain damage.[2]

Actually, I've known this for years, but it's been so damnably hard to explain just why or how this happens that I've been reluctant to publish. Nonetheless, there comes a point at which the evidence is so overwhelming that you pretty much have to vote guilty even though you can't find a motive. And the case against snow has gotten to that point. Somehow, some way[3] the white stuff messes up the gray matter.

My first intimation that snow could have a deleterious effect on cognitive processes came in college.[4] That's where I encountered, "Like an army defeated, The snow hath retreated." That's Wordsworth. Honest. I remember being very impressed that prolonged exposure to snow[5] could reduce a great poet to doggerel better suited to a detergent jingle than a literature anthology.

At about the same time, I began watching my peers hobble back from ski weekends with their faces burned into red and white rac-

---

2 - No, dammit, not *that* kind of snow. We all know what *that* does to your head. I'm talking about the real kind: The falls-from-the-sky-and-lies-in-wait-on-the-sidewalk-until-you-slip-and-bruise-your-tailbone-which-hurts-like-a-sonuvabitch kind.

3 - How come you only need one word to say "somehow" but you need two words to say, "some way?" Working hypothesis: Because Noah Webster was from Connecticut, and they get a lot of snow there.

4 - Having grown up in Southern California, the sum total of my experience with snow amounted to a few struggles to defrost a refrigerator. This probably accounts for my clear-headedness today.

5 - The poem is entitled, "Written in March."

coon masks and their extremities wrapped in plaster casts. When I learned they had spent more money than I would list on my 1040 form to ride hours on a bus so they could race headlong down a slippery hillside on slats of fiberglass until their groins separated or their knee ligaments snapped, I found myself once again marveling at the power of snow to break one's will.

Somehow we've always known at a subconscious level that snow was not to be trusted. Look up "snow" in the dictionary and you're liable to find, as synonyms, "deceive," "mislead," "bamboozle," "fast talk," and "sell a bill of goods."

And what do we call snow in its individualized form? Snowflakes. Flakes! We know this stuff is up to no good, even if we can't quite figure out what it is.

So I have spent most of my adult life carefully avoiding snow. I am the designated driver for our family ski vacations. I've never understood the attraction of repeatedly falling down in the snow, and I was able to blow up my knee ligaments playing baseball before I could afford skiing, so for me, trips to Steamboat and Purgatory amount to sitting by a fire for a week, studying the Weather Channel and mumbling over snow chains like they're rosary beads. And, of course, keeping a watchful eye on the mental health of my brave little coven of skiers.

Ten years ago, I took a job with the National Hockey League and got to know a lot of Canadians. For the benefit of those of you not familiar with Canada, it's the big country north of Starbucks and south of Santa Claus. They have lots of snow in Canada. If you could run cars on snow, Canada would be the United Alberta Emirates, and all 947 Canadians would be sheikhs.[6]

The ravages of all this snow on the Canadian mind are both heartbreakingly sad and breathtakingly vivid.[7] I mean, just look at the games they play. They play ice hockey (which is more self-destructive than the charge of the Light Brigade, but does have the advantage of being easier on the horses), box lacrosse (which was invented by the Ojibway Indians as a means of killing off white settlers),

6 - It's the 2000 census; I haven't been able to find any more recent figures because no one but me cares.

7 - Pretty good turn of phrase, eh? Compare to snow-ravaged Wordsworth, supra.

rugby, and a brand of football in which there is no fair catch allowed, so making the team as a punt returner is like being assigned as night nurse in the Ebola wing. These are their games, their pastimes.

These people are maniacs. Calling their dollar coin the "loonie," — as they do — is almost redundant.

And speaking of money, go to Canada. Find something that costs $20. Give them a $20 bill. They'll give you change. Lots of change.

Snow. That's the only answer. Snow did that to them. Prolonged exposure to snow has frozen their brain cells.

Same thing happens in Scandinavia. For those of you unfamiliar with Scandinavia (in a recent standardized test, 87 percent of American ninth-graders thought Scandinavia was Michael Jackson's estate outside of Santa Barbara), it's where the reindeer live. The Vikings used to live there, but they moved because there was too much snow. Now they live in Minneapolis, which is almost as bad, and probably explains why they're in fourth place and can't even beat the icebound Packers, for crying out loud.

Prolonged exposure to snow has taken a toll on the Scandinavians. As evidence thereof, I offer the fact that a woman named Kristi Larsen has just spent two days in jail for naming her child "Gesher." The story I read says, "A mother of 14 was jailed this week in Oslo, Norway, because she refused to change the name she picked for her young son, even though it violated Norway's name law."

Well, this is just an embarrassment of riches as far as my theory of snowmindedness goes. First of all, the woman has 14 children. I would rest my case right there except that I know that form of dementia has shown up in more temperate climes than Oslo's.

So let's deal with the fact she named her child "Gesher." "Gesher," it turns out, is Hebrew for "bridge." Go ahead. Take as much time as you wish. Then give me a plausible explanation — other than snow — for naming your child "bridge."

Personally, I have no idea why anyone would want to name their child "bridge" — or "culvert," or "large public building," or "Pasadena Freeway," for that matter. But the bigger mystery to me is why in the name of King Knut, Norway's legislature would want to make it illegal.

Who in hell cares what this poor woman names her child? My God, she's got 14 of 'em: She's hardly got a lot of time to spend choosing names, now does she?

But "Norway has strict laws regulating names, including lists of acceptable first and last names." Lists of Acceptable Names! Now there's a job for you.

"And what do you do for a living, Bjorn?"

"Oh, I work for the Acceptable Names Bureau. First Directorate: Last Names (Hard to Pronounce, Too French-Sounding and Just Plain Silly)."

"No kidding. Sounds like hard work. Especially the French part."

"Yes, well it is pretty taxing, but at least I have the satisfaction of knowing my work is important."

I'll say it's important. How would they ever find enough work for Norwegian judges without lawsuits like this one?

Mrs. Larsen not only lost at trial, but, according to the story, "lost repeated appeals." What an absolutely fascinating case. They must be lined up around the block for a chance to write that opinion.

This required her to go "to prison Monday in Fredikstad, 50 miles south of Oslo, leaving her husband and 10 children at home[8] while she served two days in jail."

Two days in jail! For a mother of 14! The University of Texas football team was quarterbacked two weeks ago by a guy named "Major Applewhite." In Norway, his parents would have gotten the death penalty.

But just when I'd decided my theory of snow-induced lunacy was irrefutable, I came across the story of a Finnish driver named Jaakko Rytsola, who was recently ticketed for going 40 mph in a 25 mph zone. According to Time magazine, his fine was $71,400.[9]

This is because the snow-wracked brains of the Finnish legislature have come up with a system of traffic fines that is based on income. So help me. This guy Rytsola is an Internet magnate. His last traffic ticket, for a dangerous lane change, cost him $44,100.

That's $115,000 for a couple of one-point violations. I think that's just brilliant. I think we ought to get the Legislature to hold a session at Squaw Valley to consider a similar law for California. Think how much safer our world would be if we didn't have Jose Canseco and Brad Pitt and a bunch of nameless Internet millionaires in Ferraris

---

8 - The other four moved to Minneapolis.

9 - I'll pause now while you go back and re-read the entire paragraph, thinking you must have misunderstood something.

racing down the Interstate.

What a great idea! This might even augment some of the Lotto money that somehow has failed to allow our schools to buy post-War textbooks. Finland has a literacy rate of something like 99.44 percent.

I can only assume that after centuries of snow exposure the Finns have developed a couple of idiot savants whom they've elected to the legislature. In the immortal words of Billy Joel, "You may be right; I may be crazy. But it just may be a lunatic you're looking for."

We're gonna need truckloads of the stuff. ❖

— January 2002

Uff Da

How Norwegians say 'indeterminate sentencing'

My mother is Swedish and German. When I was a boy, anxious to find out what it meant that I had Swedish and German heritage, I asked her to tell me about Swedes.

"Swedes," she said, having just had a falling-out with her father, "are the most stubborn people on earth."

I didn't know quite what to make of that. Being the "most" at something seemed good, especially when it covered the entire planet. It sounded like a championship of some sort. But the few times I'd heard the word "stubborn," its context had convinced me it was not a good thing.

A few days later, I asked her about Germans. "Germans," she said, "are even more stubborn than Swedes." [1]

I struggled a little with this information. It seemed to conflict somewhat with the "World's Greatest Stubbornness" title I'd already awarded the Swedes. But if there was room in Mom's head for one group to be the most stubborn on earth and another group to be more stubborn, I determined there would be room in my head, too.

My emulation of my mother in this regard has left me with a mind

---

1- I can only assume my grandmother, whose family tree included a lot of "Zangers" and "Schneiders" and people named "Otto" had sided with her Swedish husband in whatever dispute he'd had with my mother two days earlier.

many in the bar consider distressingly capable of accommodating conflicting ideas. This has led them, over the years to describe me as either "an original thinker, unfettered by dogma," [2] or "erratic as hell," [3] depending upon whether I had ruled for them or against them.

It seems my mother unwittingly imbued me with the most important shared characteristic of all appellate judges. Having now spent five years reading petitions for rehearing filed on cases written by me and my colleagues, I realize we all share this one character trait: We all have minds that are somehow blind to the obvious incompatibilities of diametrically opposed ideas. At one time or another, we all demonstrate the ability to conceive of "most" being exceeded by "even more." Were it not for the ability of appointments secretaries to winnow out seven of us at a time who have overcome this problem and elevate them to the state Supreme Court, California law would be chaos.

Which reminds me of something else Mom taught me. "As goofy as the Swedes are, the Norwegians are even worse." I offer this both as advice for those who would petition the California Supreme Court for hearing after being denied rehearing in our court, and as explanation for an article I just read in The Wall Street Journal.

Seems the Norwegians have the same problem we've struggled with here in California for years: not enough prison space. In California, we "solve" the problem by building more prisons.[4]

Norway, however, has taken a different approach to the problem of having too many criminals and not enough criminal containers. They put the criminals on a waiting list. That's right. A waiting list. A "queue," as they so quaintly put it.

The Wall Street Journal informs me that fully half the Norwegian population of convicted criminals is walking the streets waiting for a bed to open up in prison. Without any idea when that bed will become available.

Norwegian sentencing hearings must be as confusing as my early conversations with my mother:

---

2 - I loved that one.

3 - That one, not so much.

4 - To my mind, it is a sign that cultural evolution has peaked and started back downhill when you find yourself with more prisons than drive-in movies, but that does seem to be our predicament in California.

"I find you guilty and I sentence you to three years in prison. You're free to go."

"I beg your pardon, sir?"

"You're free to go."

"I'm sorry, sir. Didn't you just find me guilty and sentence me to three years in prison?"

"Yes, I did, but we're a little booked up right now. You'll just have to wait. We'll let you know when we have room for you. Leave your home phone with the bailiff on your way out, please. Next?"

"Excuse me, sir … uh … just when might that be? That you have room for me?"

"Hard to say. Depends on how many people do worse stuff than you. Could be weeks, could be years. Next?"

The Journal article includes the story of Vidar Sandli, who was sentenced to three years in prison for possessing 4 1/2 pounds of hashish. By the time they sent him his letter telling him to report to prison THE NEXT DAY, his crime was five years old. He had married, bought a house and had a child. He was Ozzie Nelson, for crying out loud.

And he had not told his wife about his conviction. He called her at the office when he got his "Get Into Jail Now" letter and suggested she come home for lunch because he had something to tell her. Apparently he felt the news that he was a convicted dope dealer and would be leaving for prison THE NEXT DAY might require more time than was available between dinner and "Trading Spaces." [5]

Can you imagine? The next day. How do you suppose this happens on such short notice? A death? An escape? "Dear Mr. Sandli, we are pleased to inform you that a serial murderer escaped yesterday, so we have room for you now. Please report tomorrow to Devil's Armpit State Prison to begin serving your three-year sentence. We would appreciate it if you would show up two hours early for your appointment, to complete the necessary paperwork."

Needless to say, they see things differently in Norway than we do here.[6] "Nils Christie, a criminologist at the University of Oslo, calls

---

5 - Okay, here's today's redeeming social value. Hold this thought in your mind: No matter how badly things go for you today, you can take solace in the idea that at least your spouse didn't call you and tell you he/she is going to prison tomorrow for three years.

6 - No surprise to my mother.

the queue 'a sign of a civil and humane society because it indicates that most criminals are ordinary people, able to wait in line just like other people.'"

Excuse me? Able to wait in line? I spent 15 years as a prosecutor and now I've spent another 15 hearing criminal cases as a judge. My experience is that a great number of criminals are criminals precisely because they AREN'T "able to wait in line just like other people." The concept of "delayed gratification" is not big in the criminal community.

But more important than that, I'm not sure I see this as something a "humane society" comes up with. Sounds more like something Rod Serling or Stephen King would have dreamed up.

I mean, suspend for a moment your feelings about whether our prison system or any other is "humane," and tell me which seems to you to be less humane: telling someone he has to go to prison, or telling someone he has to go to prison, but we won't tell him when?

Imagine the predicament of poor Ole or Thor or Anders, who's been convicted of fraud and sentenced to six months. His conviction makes him perfect for a job as a television evangelist, but his prospective employer, just before hiring him, sees that he's going to need six months off sometime in the near future to go break rocks at the big house. Six months will almost certainly include either Christmas or Easter, and that's the busy season. We can't have that. The job offer evaporates and poor Ole/Thor/Anders finds himself back on a street corner running a game of three-card monte until the prison board finds room for him or he hears back on his job application to the insurance company.

Not to mention the effect this must have on victims. True story, related by the Journal: "Eva Frivold, a lawyer in Askim, said one of her clients was beaten by her husband, who got a sentence of several months in prison. Before reaching the front of the queue, the man attacked the woman again, forcing her to flee to a women's shelter."

Well, duh!

"You, sir, are a scummy wife-beater. I find you guilty and I sentence you to prison. Now go home to your wife until we find room for you."

Good luck trying to "preserve the domestic tranquility" with sentences like that.

Yet the Norwegians can't understand their burgeoning crime rate.

According to the Journal, "In the past four years, the line of convicts waiting to do their time nearly tripled to 2,762 — roughly the same size as the entire Norwegian prison population of 2,900 inmates." One of their judges is quoted as lamenting the fact that even in his little town near the Swedish border, "There's more violence, more drugs, more thefts … more stubbornness." [7]

How can this surprise them?

Posit Brunhilde.[8] Brunhilde is tired of waiting to be rich. She doesn't know any Norwegian criminologists, so she doesn't know she's capable of waiting her turn "just like other people." So she decides to steal something. She analyzes the possibilities. If she gets away with it, she will have what she has now plus what she stole and she will be out of prison. If she gets caught, she will have what she has now, and she will be out of prison. If she doesn't steal, she will have what she has now, and she will be out of prison. The downside of theft is so attenuated as to be damned near invisible.

Especially when you consider what Norwegian prisons must be like. The Journal says, "One Norwegian prison in Bastoy is on an island where inmates live in wooden cottages and can fish, raise vegetables and cook out."

We have those, too. We call them vacation homes, and only the wealthy can afford them.

Especially vacation homes on islands. Those are pretty much the exclusive preserve of CEOs. Which, when you consider what they did to get them, suggests to me that maybe the Norwegians aren't too far from our system of penology after all. We both put criminals on islands where they fish and cook out. The difference is the Norwegians convict them first.

Thanks to my mother, I know what this means. The United States has the worst penal system in the world. And Norway's is worse. ❖

— August 2003

---

7 - Actually, I made up the part about stubbornness, but I'm sure that a town near the Swedish border would have a lot of it, based on what Mom told me.

8 - A sentence I feel confident has never previously been written.

Food Fight!

It takes some crust to claim a patent on a peanut butter and jelly sandwich

'**T**he ideas gained by men before they are 25 are practically the only ideas they shall have in their lives."

William James said that, in what was obviously one of his crankier moments. My bet would be that he was at least twice 25 when he said it. The simple fact is there are a whole helluva lot more cranky moments after 50 than before.[1]

My own crankiness can be predicted with lunar accuracy. Once a month for the past 20 years, I've faced a deadline for a column. And, having already stockpiled "practically the only ideas" I shall have in my life before I started writing this drivel, I'm starting to run low and am often hard-pressed to fill this space — wastefully or otherwise.

The problem is compounded by the fact that I am a born procrastinator. I live by the adage, "Never put off until tomorrow what — with a little effort — you can delay until a week from Tuesday." So

---

1 - Whenever I comment about life after 50, my colleague, Justice David Sills, reminds me to "Wait till you hit 60!" This is not helping to make me less cranky.

the impending deadline doesn't really show up on my radar until it's too close for missiles or anti-aircraft, and I end up throwing rocks at it — often as it recedes from view.[2]

But almost invariably, often when I'm about to throw in the towel and tell the editor I can't write the column this month because I died, my fellow man[3] provides me with something so surpassingly stupid that it makes me wonder if maybe God should have rethought the whole "I can do this in seven days" thing. Like maybe an extra afternoon working on the humans might have been well advised. Thoughts like that just have to be exorcised, and I'm grateful to The Recorder for allowing me to get them out of my system here rather than in a courtroom or an opinion.

Today's exorcism has to do with interstate commerce, patent law, unfair competition and peanut butter sandwiches — a conglomeration of ideas rarely juxtaposed as closely or as improbably as they are in this case. All you need to know to realize just how wrong the theory of human evolution is comes from one sentence in the Los Angeles Daily Journal. It says that a company in Orrville, Ohio, "contends it holds the patent for crustless peanut butter and jelly sandwiches and it intends to maintain exclusive rights to the lunchtime staple."

Yep. Patented. Peanut butter and jelly. You got a license? If not, you better get your kids ready for the idea that Mom and Dad are gonna be doing a stretch at Leavenworth, because Menusaver Inc. is not an outfit to be trifled with.

Just ask Albie's Restaurant. Albie's runs a couple of restaurants in Michigan, and was doubtless more than a little nonplussed to receive a cease-and-desist notice from Menusaver that informed it that Menusaver holds the patent on crustless peanut butter and jelly sandwiches and would haul Albie's into court to protect that patent.

Think about that: A corporation in another state sends you a letter saying it has come to its attention that you're selling crustless PBJs and if you don't cut it out,[4] they're gonna sue your butt.

---

2 - More than once an editor has called to ask whether I've decided this month to forgo the column entirely and just phone the readers personally.

3 - I choose this term purposefully: Women produce distressingly little grist for my mill. I think they just aren't trying.

4 - Or, in this case, stop cutting it off.

I'll betcha the first thing the owner of Albie's did was look around the restaurant and try to identify the spy. Who ratted on him? Who told Menusaver he was serving crustless PBJs?

The second thing had to be this incredible Jim Carrey double-take when he realized, "Wait a minute! You can't patent peanut butter and jelly! What are these people smoking?!"

Well, it turns out you can patent peanut butter and jelly. I know this because Menusaver did it. In 1999.

NINETEEN NINETY-NINE? NINETEEN NINETY-NINE! You mean to tell me if I'd been paying attention in intellectual property class, I coulda patented peanut butter and jelly and never had to meet a deadline in my life? You mean this was just sitting out there unprotected, while moms and dads all over America failed to recognize its potential?

Apparently.

Here's what the patent describes: "The sandwich includes a lower bread portion, an upper bread portion, an upper filling and a lower filling between the lower and upper bread portions, a center filling sealed between the upper and lower fillings and a crimped edge along an outer perimeter of the bread portions for sealing the fillings therebetween."

"Therebetween!" They actually gave a patent to somebody who used the non-word "therebetween." It is inconceivable to me that states disbar lawyers every day, but will allow someone who uses the word "therebetween" in a patent application to retain his ticket.

And the patent application is for a peanut butter and jelly sandwich![5] It says, "The upper and lower fillings are preferably comprised of peanut butter and the center filling is comprised of at least jelly." [6]

That's it, folks. That's United States Patent No. 6,004,596. Owned by Len C. Kirtchman of Fergus Falls, Minn., and David Geske of Fargo, N.D. You take two pieces of bread, put peanut butter on each of them, put jelly in the middle, put the bread together so none of

---

5 - I'm pretty sure this is the most exclamation points I've ever used in a column. I don't much care for exclamation points, but I can't figure out a way to SHOUT in print.

6 - "At least jelly!?" At most, what? Jelly and pate de foie gras? Jelly and motor oil? Jelly and a diamond bracelet?

the filling is on the outside, and voila! This, the government of the United States of America considers worthy of patent protection.

True, Messrs. Kirtchman and Geske have come up with the idea of crimping the edges of the bread to keep the filling from falling out. Apparently when the ice fishing in Fergus Falls tapered off, Lenny and Dave sat around playing with their sandwiches and decided crimping was just the thing to make them better. "Hey, Lenny, lookee here what I did. You smash the edges of the sandwich, it gets all doughy and flat, eh? Pretty cool, eh?"

You think this is the idea that impressed the patent examiners? Tell you what. You go home tonight, you make a PBJ. You cut off the crusts. Then you try to crimp the edges to keep the peanut butter and jelly from falling out. Then, after you've cleaned up, you hand the resultant three-bite hors d'oeuvre to your 6-year-old and see how impressed she is.

But a patent's a patent, I guess, and although this one seems patently absurd, it's gonna take a federal district court to sort it out. That's right. That's how it ended up in the Daily Journal. They've made a federal case out of a peanut butter and jelly sandwich.

It's going to be heard on Menusaver's home court — so to speak — the U. S. District Court in Bay City, Mich. Way out there on the edge of the mitten. Bay City is what would get in your way if you were a moose trying to follow the Saginaw River to Lake Huron.[7]

You wanna know what kinda place Bay City is? Here are the other headlines from The Bay City Times the day the PBJ story broke: "Alfalfa Cooperative Files for Bankruptcy," "Au Gres Township Decides to Resurvey for Water Project," and "Councilman Sentenced for Stealing Wallet." [8]

This hardly seems the proper venue for anything as important as PBJ. But, then again, the Scopes Monkey Trial was held in Dayton, Tenn., and Jack Dempsey fought Fred Werner in Durango, Colo. At least we don't have to worry about the judge who oversees this awesome conflict doing too much partying. And Dave and Lenny can drive on over from Blizzard Central in their Suburbans, eh?

I figure the rest of us will just teeter on the edge of bankruptcy,

---

7 - I don't know; why do moose do anything?

8 - I oughta move to Bay City; those all sound like columns to me.

waiting to find out if we're gonna owe back royalties to Menusaver. My parents aren't too concerned. Mom always refused absolutely to cut crust off my sandwiches. I don't know whether she was offended by the waste or thought I ought to get used to the cold, hard cruelty of the real world right then and there, but crusts were left on at our house.[9]

But I am a serial crust-nipper. All of my kids, Bill, Megan and Caitlin, ate their PBJs without crusts. Made them happy and gave me a nice little taste of peanut butter and jelly every time I made a sandwich. Seemed like a nice tradeoff at the time. Now it means I'm probably gonna have to sign over the 4Runner and my hip-waders to Dave and Lenny.

I wonder if they got this idea before they were 25.

— March 2001

---

9 - First they were left on the bread, then they were left on the plate.

Evolution, Schmevolution

Maybe those folks in Kansas got it right after all

Mohandas K. Gandhi is supposed to have been asked after a trip to Europe what he thought about Western civilization. According to the story, he responded that he thought it would be a good idea.

I'm not sure he'd still feel that way. I have a feeling that if the same question were posed to Gandhi today, he'd say, "Can't be done; tear it down and build a bowling alley."

Certainly, I'm reaching the point of despair. I have a theory that you can measure the health of a society by the kinds of laws it finds it necessary to pass. By that measure, we are one sick bunch of puppies.

Case in point: Pick up your Penal Code, go to the pocket part, and peruse new Penal Code Section 647(k)(2), effective Jan. 1. On second thought, don't bother; I'll tell you what it says. It says it is now illegal to take pictures up a woman's skirt.[1]

Honest. The great state of California, land of the free, home of the

---

1- Now you're probably gonna have to go get the Penal Code after all, just because you don't believe me.

weird, has found it necessary to begin the new millennium by enacting legislation prohibiting one gender from surreptitiously taking pictures of the other gender's underwear. It's like fourth grade all over again, isn't it?

The impetus for this legislation comes from Southern California. Orange County, to be exact. I think most of us could have guessed this without using up one of our lifelines.

I mean, this is my home and I love it, but it is still the world''s largest open-air insane asylum. There's something in that inversion layer — the one that holds the smog down — that also keeps craziness from dissipating into the ozone.

In this case, the craziness was trapped inside the head of a 23-year-old man who was shoving a camera bag with a hidden camcorder onto the ground beneath women watching the parade at Disneyland. This enabled him to make movies under their skirts. Security guards caught him, confiscated his videotape of 30 women's undergarments, and triumphantly presented him to the Anaheim Police Department, only to find out there was nothing to charge him with. They couldn't find a law he'd violated.

APD was not amused. Cops learn to deal with the quirks and singularities of the criminal law. But they're pretty confident they know a crime when they see one. And this just had to be a crime.

But not according to California law. They went through the Penal Code, the Civil Code, the Health and Safety Code, the Harbors and Navigation Code, the Morse Code, the Code of Hammurabi, and the Codex Leicester.[2] Nothing. Nada. Zip, zilch, zero, bupkis. After more hours of reading, discussing, arguing and watercooler-kicking than anyone wants to admit, they had to let the guy go.

But it turns out this isn't just one wacko. This is what Arlo Guthrie would call "a movement." According to The Orange County Register, "there's an entire fetid subculture of these so-called upskirt photographers with various Internet sites hawking pictures and sophisticated concealed camera equipment to the furtive little creeps who like that sort of stuff."[3]

This is not encouraging. I read The Origin of Species. I don't re-

---

2 - All right, they didn't really check the Codex Leicester, but I thought if I put da Vinci into the column you could apply for MCLE credits.

3 - I like the Register. They speak clearly and you seldom have to ask how they feel about something.

member anything in there about the process of evolution backing up. I just always assumed we were going to get progressively better and smarter until we all became Tom Hanks and Oprah Winfrey. Apparently I didn't read closely enough. It's beginning to look like the evolutionary process peaked somewhere around 1954, and it's been downhill ever since.

Nor is it just my gender that's making up creepy crimes. Just the other day, the Los Angeles Times greeted me with the news that many nail salons are using methyl methacrylate[4] (rather than the much safer ethyl methacrylate[5]), which, according to the Times, has been denounced as a "poisonous and deleterious substance" by the Food and Drug Administration.[6] Because MMA is about 15 times cheaper than EMA, unscrupulous nail salon owners are subjecting their customers to "fungal infections, nail deformities, and other problems."

Now this story is just full of evidence of devolution. First, the L.A. Times thinks the story is worth front-page exposure and 56 column inches of text. By comparison, the president's State of the Union address merited 61, and a story about a major government economic report regarding inflation was worth 26.

Four-and-two-thirds feet of reportage seems like a lot of ink to be devoted to fingernail problems. I don't think this story gets that much attention in a society where Pamela Anderson Lee's plastic surgeries, marriages and videotapes aren't lead stories on the six o'clock news. If we were really evolving, this would have stopped being front-page news in the sixties.

But if this is big news — and, having never had so much as a manicure, I really can't pretend to certainty in my estimation of its import — it's pretty disturbing that California's 9,348 nail and hair salons[7] are policed by 15 inspectors, empowered to levy only a $25 fine for this sort of thing. Doesn't look like we'll be cleaning up the problem anytime soon.

But the absolute proof that the Apocalypse is nigh is the opening

---

4 - "MMA" to us fingernail cognoscenti.

5 - That would be "EMA." Try to keep up.

6 - Which, of course, would be the "ASPCA."

7 - There's a statistic you'll probably be able to use in your next brief. Turns out we didn't need the da Vinci reference for MCLE credit.

sentence of the Times story: "Last year U.S. women spent more than $4 billion on artificial fingernails. ..." Four billion dollars. Billion. With a "b."

Women did that. I'm used to my gender acting like a bunch of nut-cakes. That's why we have laws like Penal Code Section 647(k)(2). But I count on women to introduce a modicum of sanity into my daily life. If the smart gender is spending $4 billion on fingernails, what hope is there for us men? For that matter, what hope is there for the species?

Not much, judging from an article in Of Counsel magazine. According to Professor Judith F. Daar of Whittier Law School, one Ron Harris has set up a Web site on which he is selling eggs. Human eggs.

Mr. Harris, whose qualifications as a geneticist consist of work as a Playboy photographer and horse breeder, is auctioning the eggs of models and actresses.[8] According to Professor Daar, "Just log on to ronsangels.com and you too can bid on the eggs of an 'actress' whose finest moment was playing the part of a dead body on 'Homicide: Life on the Streets' and whose sole self-proclaimed defect is that she exercises too much."

That's true, you can. I did. Log on, that is, not bid.[9] I mean, just what do you do with these things? In vitro fertilization is not exactly a do-it-yourself project.

At least it shouldn't be. But if you go to ronsangels.com, which bills itself as the "most visited egg donation site in the world," you have a chance to do this most important business with a man who explains his life philosophy in a lengthy essay which includes this lovely piece of philosophical prose: "O.J. is big and black, Nicole was small and blond. His kids are better off lighter and smaller, her kids would be better off bigger and darker. Biological [sic] they were prefect [sic] for each other. Just look at their kids, there [sic] beautiful. In mathematical terms it is called 'regression of the mean.' Everything folds back on itself, otherwise we would become giants or midgets in a few generations."

Say what?

---

8 - Mr. Harris touts himself as "The King of Soft Porn." I'll bet your gynecologist's title can't match that.

9 - Jeez, I'm evolving into Dr. Suess. Read those three sentences again and tell me they don't sound like something out of The Cat in the Hat.

Of course, if you expect this kind of profound professionalism, you have to be ready to play in the big leagues, financially. The prices I saw ranged from $15,000 to $50,000 per egg. But for that price, Mr. Harris provided all the really important information: age, photograph, measurements … and cup size.

Cup size! We got people selling human eggs on the Internet based on the donor's cup size!

We got laws against this? Apparently not. Professor Daar says it's not covered by the Fertility Clinic Success Rate and Certification Act of 1992, and the boys at the Anaheim Police Department couldn't find anything in any of their codes to cover this either.

And maybe there shouldn't be. Maybe we should allow people to be as stupid as they want. Certainly we do every November.

But as long as we need to keep coming up with laws to regulate non-consensual skirt-peeping, a $4 billion fingernail industry, and reproductive assistance from "The King of Soft Porn," we can't really adhere to all this evolution nonsense, now can we? ❖

— March 2000

Tommie: The Rock Oprah Episode

Texans have strange ideas about what "well-adjusted" means

The biggest drawback to being an appellate court justice is that it makes it harder to be young. People keep asking you to swear them in and give commencement addresses and mentor their daughters.

These are not young person activities. And no matter how fresh my senior prom still is in my own mind, the fact remains that it predates about 40 pages of my daughter's seventh-grade history book.

More and more these days, I get the feeling I may have lost a step. Nothing serious, mind you. I can still go from first to third on a single to center. But I find myself with increasing frequency unable to come up with a good reason why I'd WANT to.

I've been trying to reassure myself that this is a matter of maturity, that I am finally growing up, rather than just growing older. "If the world seems to be moving a little rapidly," I've told myself, "it's only because I am learning to appreciate a more measured cadence."

I've taken solace in the thought that a more reasoned pace would result in refinement of my tastes. I'd develop an affinity for cognac and stop drinking diet cokes and "virgin coladas." I'd learn to forgo

Cajun music and Vachel Lindsay and chocolate chip cookie dough in favor of Humperdinck[1], Wordsworth, and vin et fromage.

And I just kind of assumed the rest of the world would move right along with me at roughly the same pace. This seemed to me to be the natural order of things: a long slow progression into eventual — but still distant — geezerhood.

Wrongo-bongo, Beds; wake up and smell the latte. That roaring sound you hear is the 21st century flying down the track like a bullet train on meth, and it's gonna flatten you without even feeling the bump.

It appears that the rest of society has no intention of either slowing down or growing up. They're out there carousing and debauching and just generally flouting convention in ways my poor, straight little mind never conceived of. To borrow from a friend of mine, "Them folks are eatin' things we wouldn't even go swimmin' with back home."

I was informed by my radio this morning that police in San Diego had to respond to a call of a "man beating his chicken."[2] Right away, I knew this guy's having more fun than I am. In my whole life, I have never beaten a chicken.

When they answered the call, police found this guy had tied the chicken up (Honest!), sat him in a box of water (the chicken, not the guy), and was kneeling in front of him, spitting in his face and hollering insults.[3]

Picture that. Just put down your coffee for a minute and work up a clear mental image of that entire tableau. Then tell me how in the world he ever thought that up.

Some folks just know how to have a good time.

I, on the other hand, clearly lack the imagination necessary to keep up with modern measures of "fun." I have no tattoos. I have no earrings. I have no nose rings, eye rings, nipple rings or tongue studs.[4]

I don't eat sushi unless it's first dipped in batter and then deep-

---

1 - The original, not the Vegas one.

2 - Sounded like a euphemism to me, too, but it wasn't.

3 - Sounds a lot like some calendar courts I've appeared in.

4 - If you can read the phrase, "nipple rings or tongue studs" without shuddering, you are considerably better prepared for this century than I am.

fried. I've never had an espresso or a cappuccino or a latte or any-thing else, the essence of which is boiled coffee beans. The only way I'm ever going into a Starbuck's or a Diedrich's is if Bob Seger does a concert in one of them.

I don't do drugs, I don't smoke, I don't drink — except, of course, for tequila, and that isn't so much drinking as it is reupholstering your esophagus. My idea of an alternative lifestyle is someone who holds the TV remote in the LEFT hand.

I did not watch a single episode of "Survivor."

And, incredible as it may seem to those of you who've seen me, no part of my body has ever been surgically enhanced.[5]

For all these reasons, I am resigned to my place in the après garde of modern culture. I accept the fact that I enjoy a lifestyle which, by today's standards, is hardly deserving of the suffix "style."

Nonetheless, I wrote the chicken guy off as an aberration. People who beat chickens are, to my mind, the cannon fodder of the cultur-al advance. I figured he was far enough ahead of the rest of us troops that he might actually have been the rear guard of the last Grateful Dead concert.

But then I read about Jerry Lee Tommie. I read about Jerry Lee Tommie in the opinions of the Texas Supreme Court. The opinions of the Texas Supreme Court are a good starting point any time you're looking for stories about people with entirely too many first names.[6]

In a memorandum opinion, the Texas Supreme Court affirmed the judgment of the Texas Court of Civil Appeals, which had reached the remarkable opinion that Jerry Lee Tommie was both "happy" and "well-adjusted." Since these are not the kind of conclusions courts of appeal are typically called upon to render, it should come as no sur-prise to you that *Connecticut General Life Insurance Co. v. Tommie,* 619 S.W.2d 199, is not a typical case.[7]

Here are the facts of *ConGenLifeInsCo v. Jerry Lee,* as related in the official reporter:

---

5 - Although my breastbone was wired together after the heart surgery, and I do have a metal clip in my left temporal lobe.

6 - I have a cousin in El Paso named Billy Ray Dale who is better than even-money to make the Texas Supreme Court advance sheets in any given year.

7 - Your second clue that it is not a typical case is its citation in this column. Read on for your third and final clue.

While Mrs. Tommie was out of the house shopping for groceries, Mr. Tommie dressed himself in her wig, bra, nightie and panties. He went into a bedroom and placed the end of a nylon exercise rope in a noose around his neck. He placed a pad around his neck under the rope. Standing with his back to the door he ran the other end of the rope over the top of the door and down the opposite side of the door around the outside doorknob, and then tied that end around his left foot. The exercise rope was equipped with pulleys so that with his left foot he could increase or decrease the pressure of the rope around his neck. The purpose of the preparations made by Mr. Tommie, according to the medical testimony, was to heighten sexual pleasure during masturbation by reducing the supply of blood, and therefore the supply of oxygen to the brain, by gradually tightening the rope around his neck. The reduced oxygen to the brain produces a state of hypercapnia, or an increase of carbon dioxide in the blood, and a state of hypoxia, or a decrease in oxygen in the blood, which is supposed to increase the intensity of orgasm. 619 S.W.2d 199, 201-202, so help me.

Boy, do I feel out of it. Some East Texas redneck with three first names knows more about sex than I do.

Or at least, KNEW more about sex. Ol' Jerry Lee bit — you should pardon the expression — the big one. Something went awry with his little Howard Stern science project and he strangled himself.

When Mrs. Tommie got home, she was unable to get into the bedroom until she got a kitchen knife and cut the rope, at which time she was confronted with a picture even more difficult to imagine than the chicken guy on his knees spitting at a tied-up pullet in a tub of water. If you haven't already, go back and read the excerpt from the opinion quoted above and imagine what this poor woman's husband looked like when she found him.

So whaddya think? You think this is pretty bizarre behavior? You think this is maybe just a LITTLE bit off the wall? I did. But then, I'm Mr. Stodgy, remember?

You wanna know what the appellate courts of The Great State of Texas thought? In rejecting the idea of suicide, they opined that there was, "abundant evidence that Mr. Tommie ... was a well-adjusted, happy individual who was looking forward to the future ..." 619 S.W.2d 199, 203.

Well, of course he was. And Dennis Rodman will be the next Bishop of Rome.

Oh, I have no doubt Mr. Tommie was happy. And I'm quite sure he was "looking forward to the future." In fact, I'm reasonably certain that his rather obsessive, happy anticipation of the IMMEDIATE FUTURE was what got his ass dead. But I'm afraid I take issue with the judicial description of him as "well-adjusted."

"Well-adjusted!" And this wasn't the North American Society for the Preservation of Serious Weirdness that called him well-adjusted. This wasn't some half-baked band of peyote-chewing dingbats. This was the Texas Supreme For-Crying-Out-Loud Court. If this is what passes for "well-adjusted" in Texas these days, I'll just stay north of Red River and west of the Pecos, thank you very much.

Nonetheless, I am a trained logician[8] and if you ignore the undistributed major premise, the syllogism here is very simple — even for a rookie justice. The Texas Supreme Court is a prestigious, conservative body, and it thinks men who dress up in women's lingerie and put nylon nooses around their necks are "well-adjusted." I want to be considered "well-adjusted" by prestigious, conservative bodies.[9] Therefore …

Therefore I'm leaving the court. My life is obviously too banal and humdrum to relate to most Californians anyway, so I'm embarking upon a new endeavor.

I'm opening an escort supply service, providing chickens, lingerie, pulleys and rope to "happy, well-adjusted individual[s], looking forward to the future." That's just exactly how the ad will read.

You can come visit me when I'm rich. I'm sure I'll seem a lot younger. ❖

— October 2000

---

8 - Which I understand to be someone who performs sleight of hand with large pieces of firewood.

9 - Especially the one presided over by The Honorable Ronald George.

biographies

After 15 years as a prosecutor, **William W. Bedsworth** — "Beds" — was elected to the Orange County Superior Court bench in 1986. He was re-elected in 1992 and appointed a justice of California's Fourth

ALAN J. DUIGNAN

District Court of Appeal, Division 3, in 1997. He also has been employed for the past 11 years as a goal judge for the National Hockey League.

In addition to law review articles and serious legal pieces for publications such as Sierra and Coast magazines, he has written his humor column, "A Criminal Waste of Space," since 1981. It appears monthly in The Recorder, a San Francisco legal newspaper, and other American Lawyer Media publications, as well as Orange County Lawyer magazine and on the Web at callaw.com. A previous collection of columns, What I Saw and Heard, was published in 1996.

His wife, three children, three cats and an orchid count on him for an occasional laugh.

Illustrator **Mark Ziemann** is a San Francisco-based artist. He teaches animation and other art classes in San Francisco at The Art Institutes International. He paints, exhibits and sells his work in the San Francisco Bay Area and other cities. His Web site is www.flash.net/~zmanart.